I0446173

Nikon Z30 User Reference

A Comprehensive Companion for Mastering the Features and Functions of the Z30 Camera

By

Clyde Bertram

Copyright ©2023 Clyde Bertram,

Table of Content

INTRODUCTION

Nikon's Z30 is part of their growing mirrorless camera series. It's great for social media with features like 4k recording, a big image sensor, eye-detect autofocus, 1080p 60fps streaming, and user-friendly operation, catering to the rise of platforms like Twitch, Shorts, Reels, and TikTok.

Nikon's new camera, the z30, is designed to make it easy for beginners to create high-quality videos. Despite its simple operation, it captures excellent UHD 4k video at 30p with a large APS-C sensor, providing much better quality than a smartphone. It also features fast autofocus, a touchscreen, a red tally light, and a high-quality built-in stereo mic. If you're a new or smartphone-only content creator, the Nikon z30 is an excellent choice to consider upgrading.

The new Nikon z30 is a camera designed to make it easy to create content quickly. It has a 20.8 MP camera can shoot high-quality 4k video, giving creators professional-looking images with a nice background blur. It is possible because it has a larger sensor than a typical smartphone, performing well in low light and providing a pleasing depth of field. Additionally, if you want to slow down your content for a funny or emotional effect, the z30 can capture high-speed footage at 120 frames per second.

With you in mind, Nikon made a camera known as the Z30. Don't be scared if you're into making videos with your smartphone and worry about big cameras! The Z30 is light, only 350 grams, so it's comfy to hold for a long time and easy to carry. It's simple to use with a touch screen, and a red light shows when recording. The autofocus is smart, focusing on faces quickly, and it even works for dogs and cats. If you're showing off something, turn off the face focus, and the camera will focus on whatever you point it at.

The z30 camera can record up to 125 minutes non-stop in high-quality HD at 24 frames per second for lengthy makeup tutorials or cake recipes. If you're shooting in 4k, it can record continuously for about 35 minutes. You can also take screenshots while recording for thumbnails, and for recording sessions longer than two hours, you can use a USB-C connection for constant power.

This small camera takes excellent pictures, focuses well, and has impressive sound. The built-in stereo mic is better than the ZFC and z30. You can choose specific frequencies like vocal range for vlogging or a wider range for capturing background noise. You can also use an external microphone for a more focused sound by plugging it into the side.

This camera has a handy micro HDMI output for connecting to bigger screens or recorders, allowing for future upgrades. You can also do high-quality live streaming at 1080p 60fps using the USB-C connection, which doubles as a long-lasting power supply. It works with a specific EN/EL25 battery and uses SDXC cards in just one slot. The buttons are smartly placed, especially the record button, which is easy to reach whether you're shooting usually or in selfie mode.

If you're worried about using this camera, don't be! Nikon designed it to be easy. There's a guide in the camera that lets you pick a feature from the menu, press the question mark button, and it will explain what that feature does. It's a fantastic way to learn about the camera while taking pictures.

Nikon made it simple to adjust necessary camera settings with a shortcut called i-menu. Whether it's white balance, autofocus, or recording quality, you can easily tweak them. In making high-quality videos as a beginner, this camera is designed in such a way it will assist you. Plus, Nikon's Snapbridge app for IOS and Android lets you effortlessly share content, work in the background, and even control recording remotely.

The camera is excellent for videos but can snap high-quality 20-megapixel photos at a speedy 11 frames per second. If you're a content creator using your phone but considerig a dedicated video camera upgrade, the z30 is perfect. It's ideal for new profile pictures or thumbnails.

CHAPTER 1: GETTING THE CAMERA UP AND RUNNING

Preparing the Camera for Initial Use

After checking out the camera features, we'll talk about the different parts and what they do, which we've already covered. In this chapter, we'll teach you how to use your camera. You'll learn about the lens, putting in and taking out the battery and memory card, attaching the camera strap correctly, and charging your camera. Let's get started!

Attaching the lens

Before attaching the lens, make sure to remove the body and rear caps from both the camera and the lens. This will prevent dust or debris from entering the camera's delicate internal components.

To align the lens correctly, identify the small dot on the lens mount and align it with the corresponding dot on the camera body. Once aligned, carefully insert the lens into the camera mount, ensuring that it is properly seated.

With the lens firmly in place, slowly rotate it in a counterclockwise direction until it clicks securely into position. This locking mechanism ensures a stable and secure connection between the camera and the lens.

The lens comes equipped with a front cap that protects the delicate lens elements from scratches and dust. To remove the cap, simply grasp it firmly and pull it straight off.

Once the front cap is removed, you'll notice that the lens is initially locked in the "closed" position, indicated by the zoom indicator pointing to the "16" mark. To unlock the lens and extend its focal length, simply rotate the zoom ring towards the "50" mark.

Unlike some lenses that require a button press to unlock the zoom mechanism, this particular lens only requires a gentle push and rotation of the zoom ring. As you rotate the ring, you'll feel a slight resistance followed by a click indicating that the lens is fully unlocked.

To retract the lens to its "closed" position, simply reverse the process and rotate the zoom ring back towards the "16" mark. As you rotate the ring, you'll again feel a slight resistance followed by a click, indicating that the lens is securely locked in its retracted position.

Removing and changing the lens

To remove the lens and attach a new one, follow these steps:

1. Locate the lens release button (marked with a white dot) on the camera body, just above the Z30 symbol.
2. While holding down the lens release button, gently rotate the lens clockwise until it clicks and disengages from the camera mount.

3. Carefully set the lens aside, ensuring that the front and rear lens caps are securely attached to prevent dust or debris from entering the lens elements or camera sensor.
4. To attach a new lens, align the white dot on the lens mount with the corresponding white dot on the camera body.
5. Gently press the lens firmly into the camera mount, ensuring that it is properly seated.
6. Slowly rotate the lens counterclockwise until it clicks securely into position. This locking mechanism ensures a stable and secure connection between the camera and the lens.
7. Once the lens is attached, remove the front lens cap to prepare for shooting.

Inserting and removing the battery and memory card

On the bottom of the Nikon Z30, you'll find a battery and memory card door secured by a lock lever. To access the battery and memory card compartments, simply slide the lock lever to the side,

The battery compartment door also features a small rubber notch, specifically designed to accommodate dummy batteries. These battery blanks are used for external power sources, such as AC adapters or battery grips. The notch allows the power cord to pass through without interfering with the door closure.

Inserting and Removing the Battery

To insert the battery, follow these steps:

1. Locate the battery compartment door.

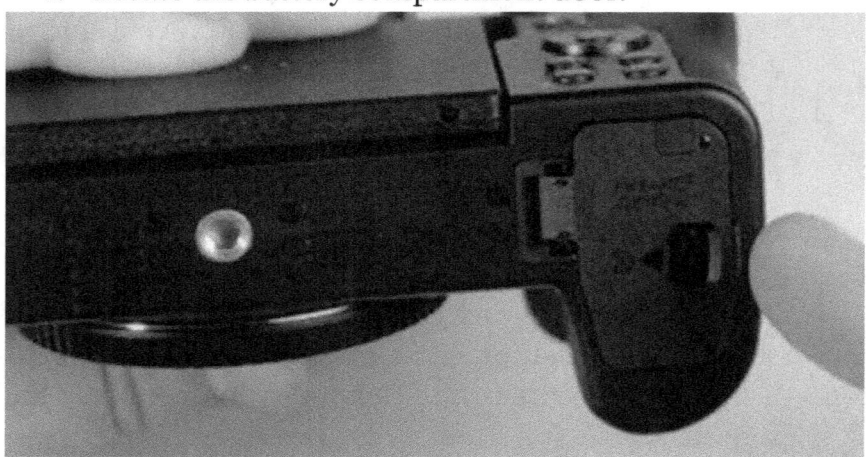

2. Slide the lock lever to the side to unlock the door.
3. Insert the battery into the compartment, ensuring it is properly aligned and seated.

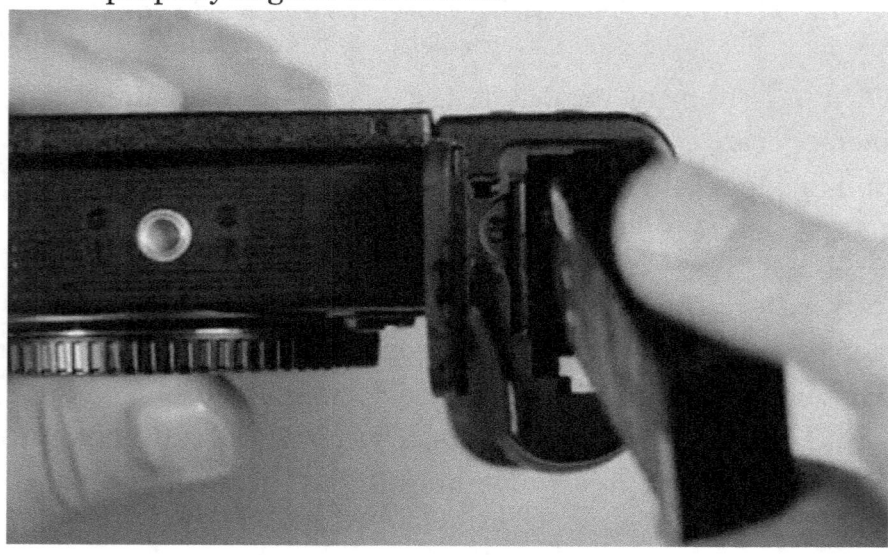

4. Slide the lock lever back to the locked position to secure the battery compartment door.

To remove the battery, follow these steps:

1. Locate the battery compartment door.

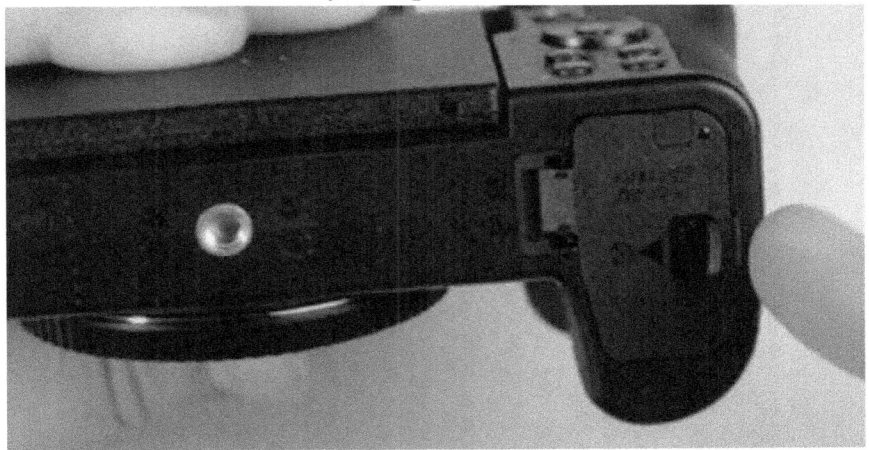

2. Slide the lock lever to the side to unlock the door.
3. Push the yellow lever located on the side of the battery compartment to eject the battery.

4. Carefully remove the battery from the compartment.

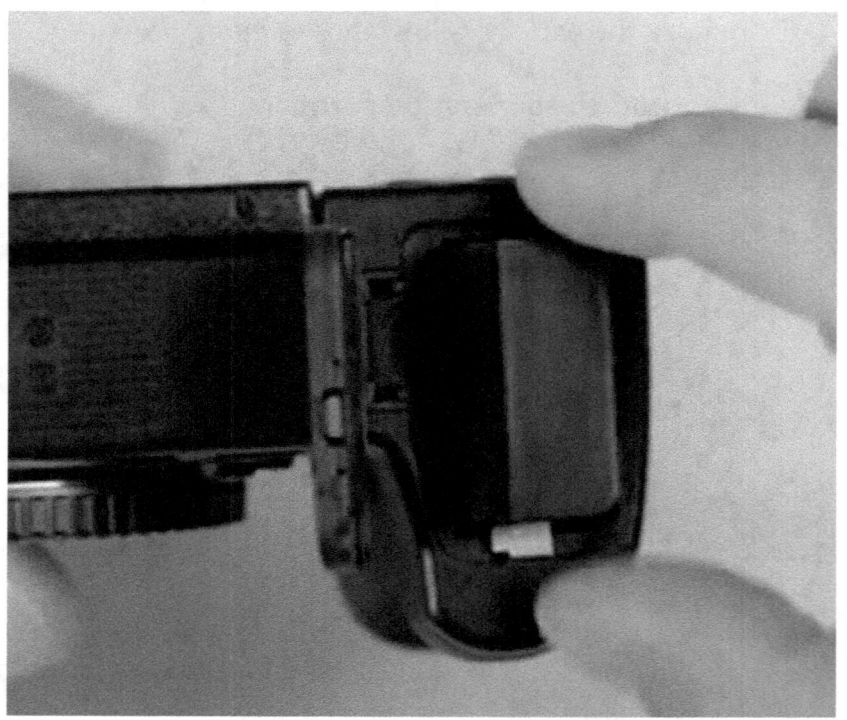

5. Slide the lock lever back to the locked position to secure the battery compartment door.

Inserting and Removing the Memory Card

To insert the memory card, follow these steps:

1. Locate the memory card slot.

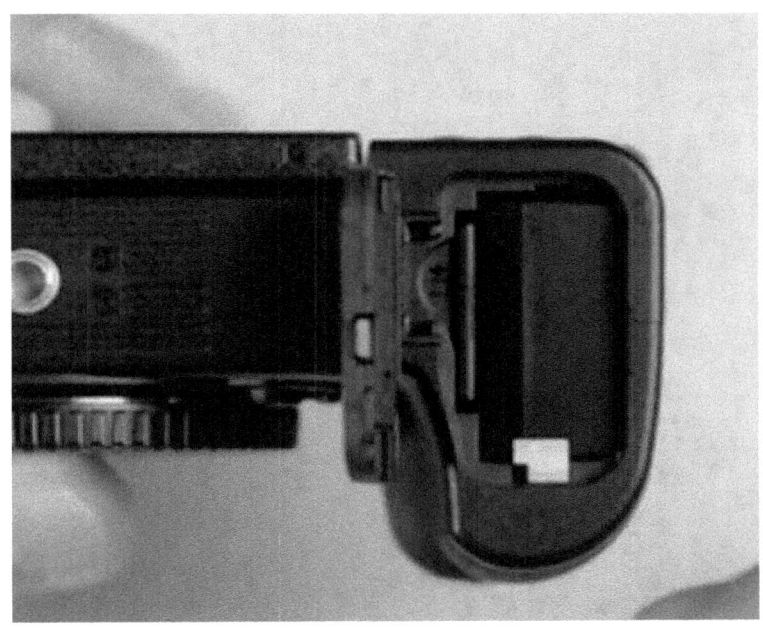

Insert the memory card into the slot, ensuring it is properly
aligned and seated. The label on the memory card should face
towards the battery.

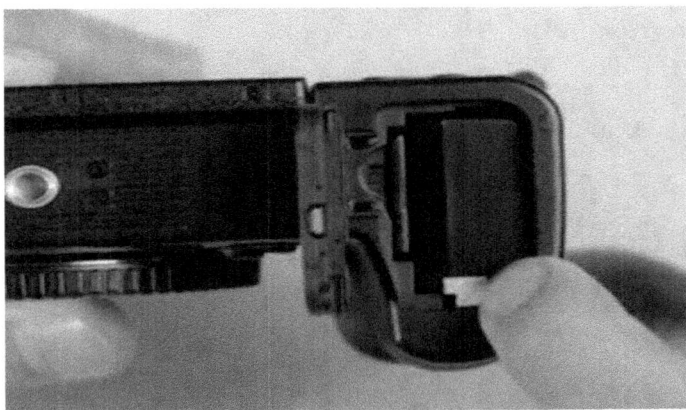

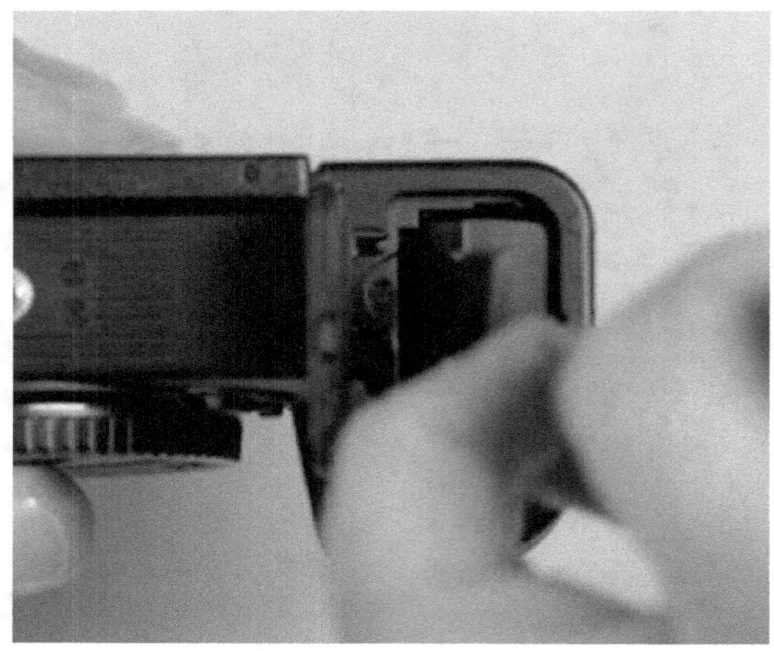

2. Push the memory card down until it clicks into place.

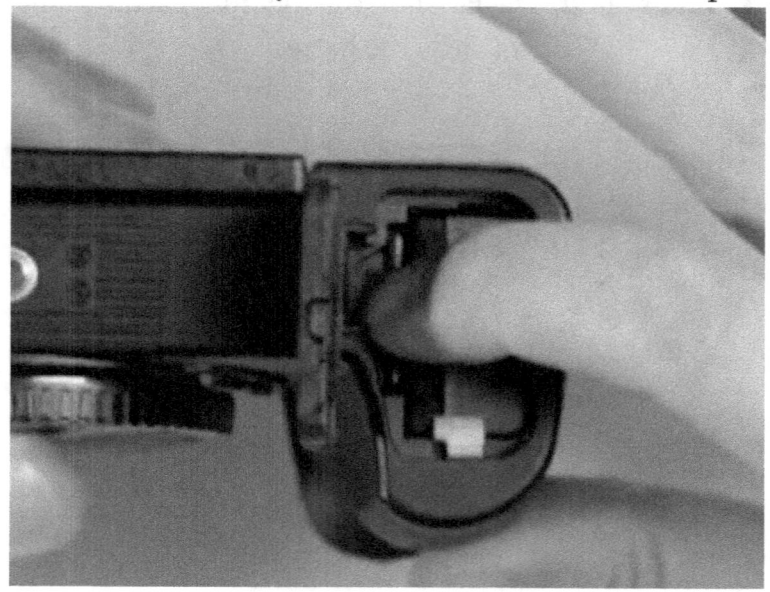

To remove the memory card, follow these steps:

1. Locate the memory card slot.

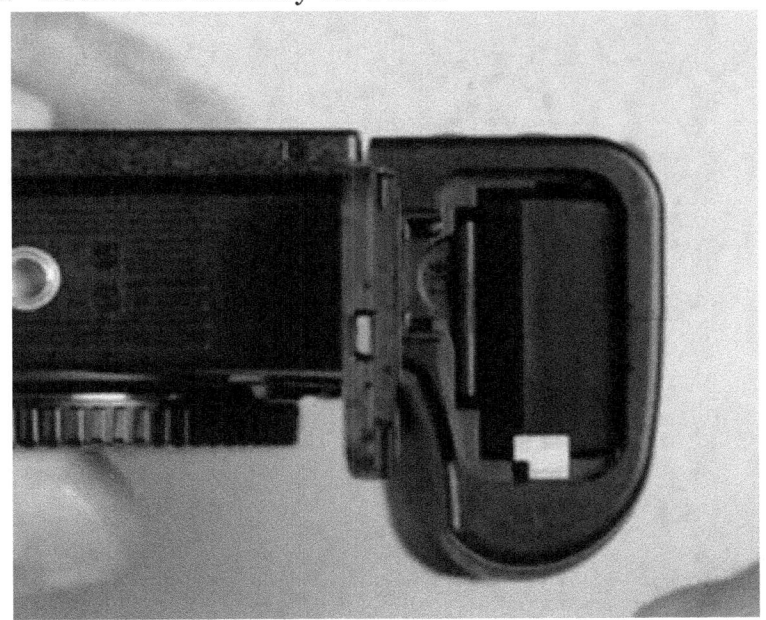

2. Gently push the memory card inwards.

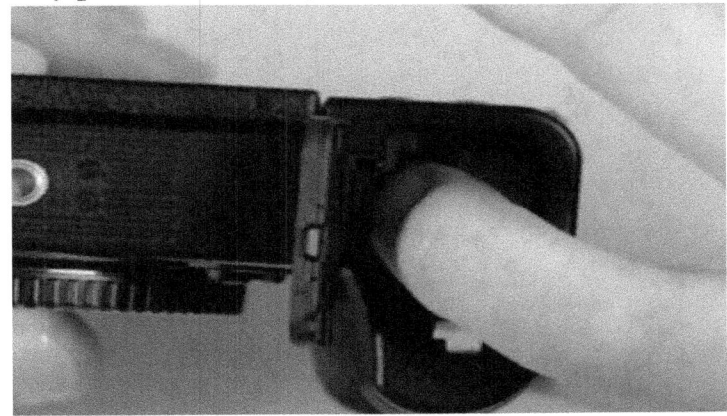

3. Release the memory card as it pops out of the slot.

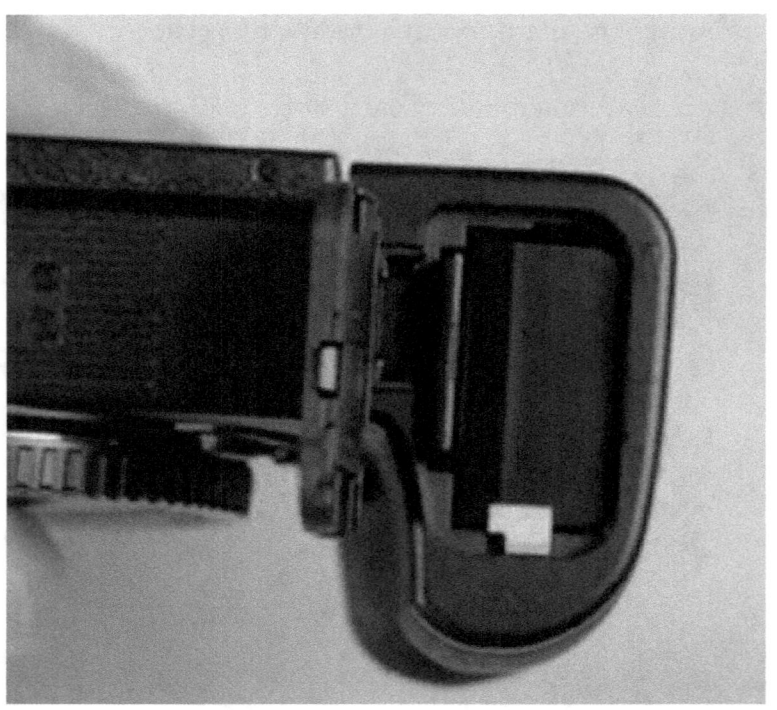

4. Carefully remove the memory card from the slot.

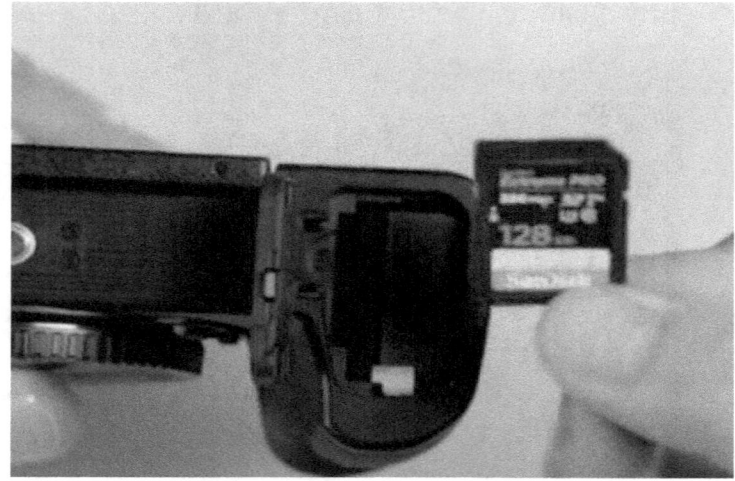

Attaching the Camera Strap

To attach the Nikon camera strap, follow these steps:

1. Locate the small collar on the end of the strap.
2. Push the collar through the strap, ensuring that the Nikon logo is facing outwards.
3. Slide the strap into the open end of the strap holder on the camera from the bottom up, not the top down.
4. Push the strap through the little collar.
5. If you need more length, pull on the strap to extend it.
6. Grab the buckle and push it inwards slightly.
7. Locate the piece of strap that you just layered underneath the buckle.
8. Pull this piece of strap up, keeping it underneath the buckle.
9. Push the strap through the bottom of the buckle.
10. You should now have a double loop.
11. Repeat steps 3 to 10 on the other side of the camera to attach the other end of the strap.
12. Tighten the strap as desired.
13. Your Nikon camera strap is now securely attached.

Exploring the camera ports and connectors

The Nikon Z30 features a variety of ports and connections that allow you to expand its functionality and connect it to external devices.

HDMI Port

The HDMI port, located on the left side of the camera, is used to connect the camera to an external monitor or television. This allows you to view your photos and videos on a larger screen, making it ideal for sharing your work with others.

USB-C Port

The USB-C port, also located on the left side of the camera, serves multiple purposes:

- **Firmware Updates:** The USB-C port is used to update the camera's firmware, ensuring you have the latest features and bug fixes.
- **Image Transfer:** You can connect the camera to your computer using a USB-C cable to transfer photos and videos directly from the camera to your computer. This method is an alternative to using an SD card reader.
- **Charging:** The USB-C port can be used to charge the camera's battery. This is particularly useful when you're on the go and don't have access to an AC outlet.

External Microphone Port

Located on the top of the camera, the external microphone port (labeled "MIC") allows you to connect an external microphone to enhance your audio recordings. This is especially beneficial for situations where you need better audio quality or want to capture specific sounds.

Speakers

The speakers are located on the front of the camera, below the external microphone port. They provide playback audio for videos and recorded audio.

SD Card Slot

The SD card slot, located on the right side of the camera, is used to store photos and videos. The camera supports UHS-I SD cards, ensuring fast data transfer speeds

Battery Compartment

The battery compartment, located on the bottom of the camera, houses the rechargeable lithium-ion battery.

External Flash Mount

Located on the top of the camera, between the speakers, is a hot shoe that can be used to mount an external flash. While the Z30 doesn't have a built-in pop-up flash, using an external flash can provide more powerful and versatile lighting options.

Charging the camera

The Nikon Z30 camera does not come with a pre-charged battery, so you'll need to charge it before using it for the first time. Nikon provides a USB-C cable and a wall charger to facilitate the charging process.

Here's how you can charge the camera:

1. Make sure the battery is inserted into the camera before connecting the charger.
2. Plug the USB-C end of the cable into the appropriate port on the camera, typically located on the left side.

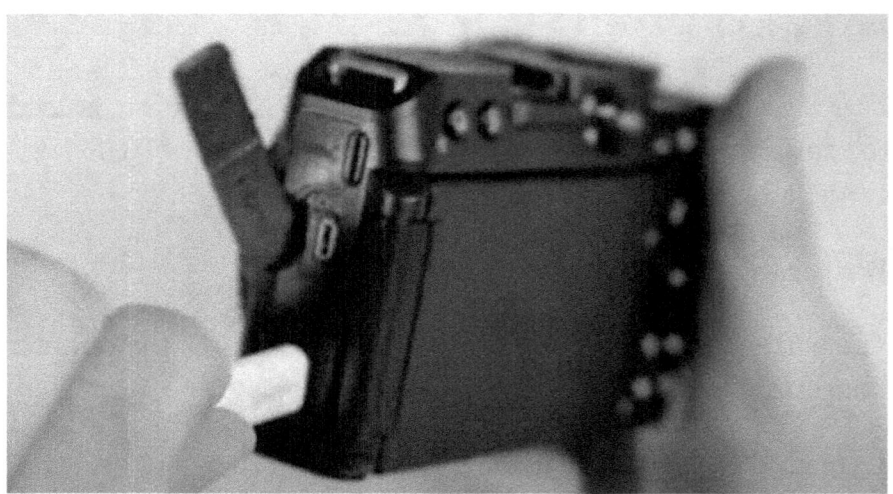

3. Connect the other end of the USB-C cable to the power brick provided by Nikon.
4. Insert the power brick plug into a standard wall outlet.
5. When the camera is connected to the charger, an orange light will illuminate on the camera body. This indicates that the battery is charging.
6. The charging process will take approximately 2 hours and 40 minutes for a completely depleted battery. Once the battery is fully charged, the orange light will turn off.

You can also charge the camera battery by connecting the camera via USB to any computer with a Type-A USB port. Simply turn off the camera, connect the USB-C cable to the camera and computer, and the battery will start charging.

Note:

- **Charging Completion Indicator**

When the battery is fully charged, the orange light on the camera body will turn off. At this point, the camera is ready to be used.

- **Battery Life**
  The Nikon Z30 has an estimated battery life of approximately 330 shots. To ensure you have enough power for extended shooting sessions, it is recommended to carry extra batteries.

Exploring External Camera Features

Topside controls

Eyelet for camera strap: This allows you to securely attach a camera strap to the camera body, making it easier to carry and preventing it from being dropped.

Focal plane mark: This is a reference point on the camera body that indicates where the film or sensor plane is located. This is important for accurately focusing your lens.

Stereo microphone: This records high-quality stereo sound, which is ideal for vlogging and other video projects.

ISO button: This allows you to quickly adjust the camera's ISO sensitivity, which affects the brightness of your photos and videos.

Power switch: This turns the camera on and off.

Shutter-release button: This takes a photo or starts and stops recording video.

Main command dial: This is used to control various camera settings, such as aperture, shutter speed, and exposure compensation.

Video-record button: This starts and stops recording video.

Mode dial: This selects the camera's shooting mode, such as Auto, Manual, or Scene.

Accessory shoe: This allows you to attach external accessories, such as a flash or an electronic viewfinder.

Speaker: This plays back audio from your videos.

Front features

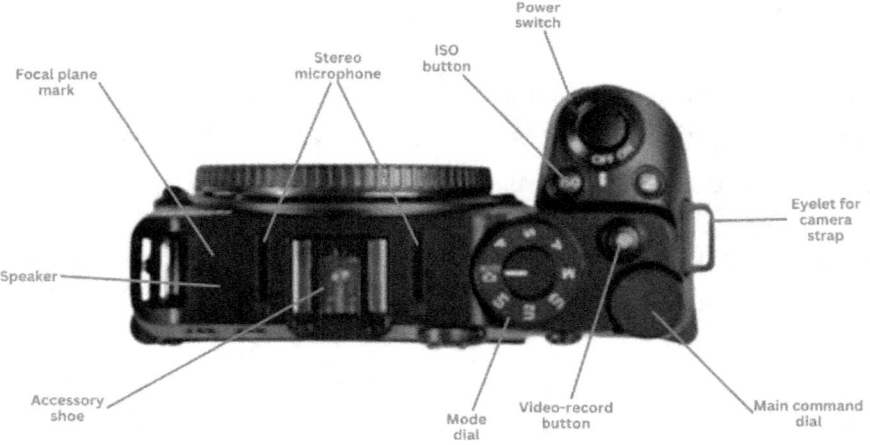

Sub-command dial: This is used to control additional camera settings, such as white balance and drive mode.

Image sensor: This is the light-sensitive chip that captures images and videos.

CPU contacts: These allow for communication between the camera's CPU and other accessories.

Lens mounting mark: This helps to ensure that the lens is mounted correctly on the camera body.

REC lamp: This illuminates when the camera is recording video.

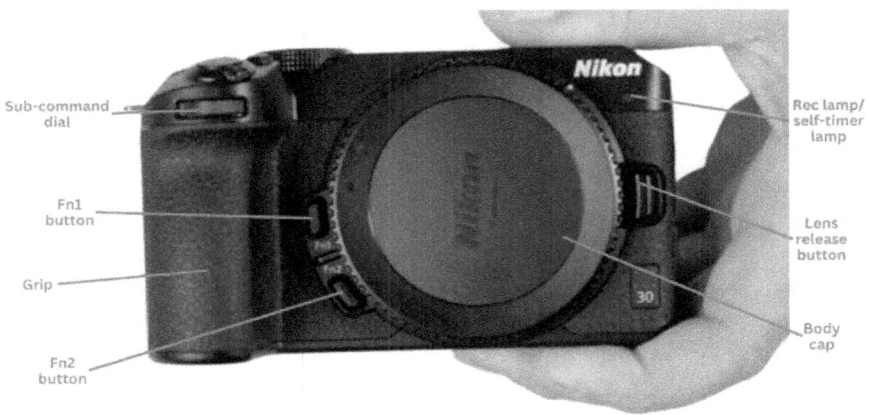

Cover for microphone connector: This protects the microphone connector from dust and debris.

Cover for HDMI and USB connectors: This protects the HDMI and USB connectors from dust and debris.

Connector for external microphone: This allows you to connect an external microphone for improved audio recording.

HDMI connector: This allows you to connect the camera to an HDTV or other compatible device.

Charge lamp: This indicates whether the camera is charging or not.

USB connector: This allows you to connect the camera to a computer for data transfer or charging.

Lens release button: This releases the lens from the camera body.

Lens mount: This is the connection point for the camera lens.

Body cap: This protects the image sensor from dust and scratches when the camera is not in use.

Fn2 button: This is a customizable function button that can be assigned to various camera settings.

Fn1 button: This is another customizable function button that can be assigned to various camera settings.

Back-of-the-body controls

DISP button: This button toggles the display of information on the camera's monitor.

Photo/video selector: This button switches between still photo and video recording modes.

AE-L/AF-L button: This button locks exposure and autofocus settings, allowing you to recompose your shot without having to worry about the camera's settings changing.

i button: This button displays the camera's shooting menu, which allows you to adjust a variety of settings.

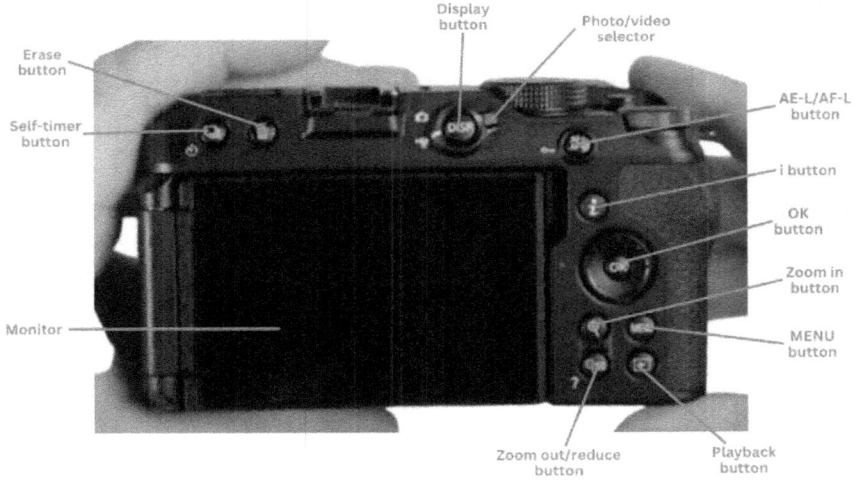

Multi selector: This control allows you to navigate through menus and select menu items.

MENU button: This button opens the camera's main menu, which provides access to all of the camera's settings.

Playback button: This button enters playback mode, allowing you to view and delete images and videos.

Zoom out/reduce button: This button zooms out on the image or video you are viewing.

Zoom in button: This button zooms in on the image or video you are viewing.

Memory card access lamp: This light illuminates when the camera is accessing the memory card.

Monitor: This is the liquid crystal display (LCD) screen on which you can view your images and videos, as well as adjust camera settings.

Self timer button: This button activates the self-timer, which delays the shutter release for a specified amount of time.

Erase button: This button deletes the selected image or video.

CHAPTER 2: CONTROLLING FOCUS AND DEPTH OF FIELD

Autofocus Types

A mirrorless Nikon camera doesn't have a separate autofocus module. Instead, it uses the camera sensor itself for autofocus. There are two types of autofocus built into the sensor:

Phase detection autofocus (PDAF)

The Nikon Z30's imaging sensor is equipped with focal plane phase-detection autofocus, employing 209 AF points arranged in a grid-like pattern that covers approximately 90 percent of the electronic viewfinder (EVF) or monitor. These AF points are strategically positioned to provide comprehensive coverage across the frame, ensuring accurate and reliable autofocus performance.

Each of the 209 AF points is composed of multiple photosites (pixels), meaning that thousands of pixels are actively involved in the autofocus process. Phase-detection AF, a highly responsive autofocus technique, operates by comparing specific areas of the subject on different parts of the sensor.

To achieve this comparison, certain rows of the sensor serve a dual purpose. These specialized rows can capture regular image data from the subject while simultaneously comparing the subject with other rows for autofocus. In essence, all sensor rows contribute to capturing image data for your photographs;

however, a select number of these rows additionally provide autofocus functionality by comparing subject areas.

This dual-purpose design enables the Z30 to maintain a high resolution image while simultaneously ensuring fast and precise autofocus performance, even in low-light conditions. The 209 AF points effectively blanket the shooting area, ensuring that the camera can quickly and accurately lock focus on your subject, regardless of their position within the frame.

The Z30's phase-detection autofocus system is particularly well-suited for capturing moving subjects. By continuously comparing subject areas across the sensor, the camera can maintain focus even when the subject is in motion. This makes the Z30 an excellent choice for sports photography, wildlife photography, and other scenarios where capturing sharp images of moving subjects is crucial.

Contrast detection autofocus (CDAF)

In addition to phase-detection autofocus, the Nikon Z30's imaging sensor also employs focal plane contrast-detection autofocus, utilizing pixel-level contrast detection for precise focusing. Unlike phase-detection autofocus, which relies on dedicated AF points, contrast-detection autofocus utilizes the entire surface of the imaging sensor to identify contrast transitions between light and dark areas.

While contrast-detection autofocus is generally slower than phase-detection autofocus, it offers exceptional accuracy due to its pixel-level operation. This form of autofocus primarily comes into play when Pinpoint AF (page 89) is selected. However, according to Nikon literature, the Z30 may also employ a subtle blend of phase-detection and contrast-detection autofocus to achieve enhanced focusing precision.

This combination of autofocus techniques enables the Z30 to deliver reliable and accurate focusing performance in various shooting scenarios, ensuring sharp and well-focused images even in challenging conditions.

Focus Mode

Focus modes help you decide how your camera focuses on things in photos and videos. If your subject is still or barely moving, there's a mode to make the camera focus and stay focused (AF-S). If your subject is moving, there's another mode that keeps adjusting focus as long as you press the Shutter-release button halfway or a specific back button down (AF-C).

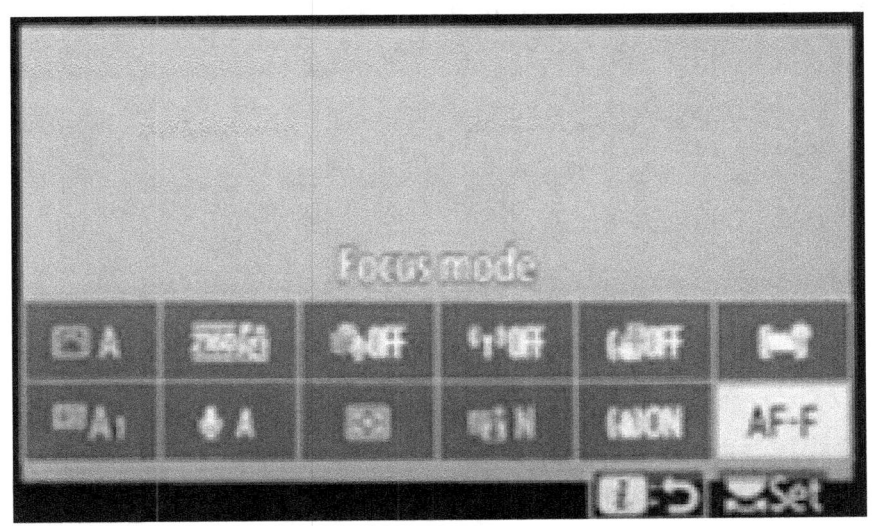

In Movie mode, the Nikon Z30 offers two focus options. With full-time autofocus (AF-F), the camera keeps adjusting focus automatically while you're recording, and you don't need to press any buttons. There's also Manual focus (MF) mode where you can manually adjust focus. To help you focus accurately, you can use focus Peaking and on-screen symbols.

Let's look at each Focus mode and figure out when and how to use them. In the examples, I'll use the i Menu access method, but keep in mind you can also use an assigned button (like Fn2) or the Photo and Movie Shooting Menus, as explained in the previous section about accessing mode groups.

In this part of the chapter, I'll talk about a pretend "Focus button." It means either pressing the Shutter-release button halfway to focus or using a specific button like AE-L/AF-L for back-button focus. Instead of repeatedly mentioning these methods, I'll use the "Focus button." So, whenever you read that, think of your preferred button and way to focus.

AF Mode Auto-Switch (AF-A) Mode

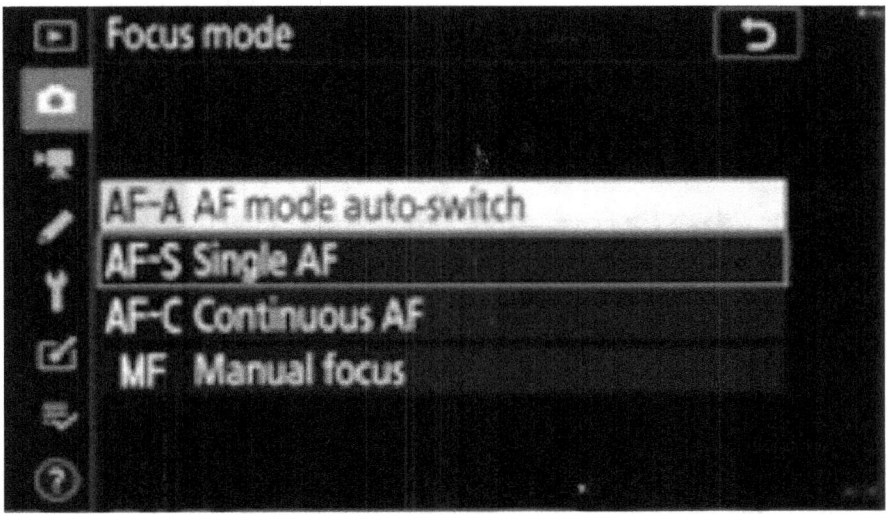

AF mode auto-switch (AF-A) is like a smart setting for your camera that automatically adjusts to whether your subject is still or moving, making it easy to capture different types of scenes.

- **The subject is not moving:** When you hit the Focus button, and your subject isn't moving, the camera stays in AF-S mode. In this mode, the focus stays fixed on the subject as long as it remains still. But if the camera sees the subject move, it switches to AF-C mode and won't lock the focus until the subject stops moving again.
- **The subject is moving:** When you tap the Focus button and your subject is moving, the camera switches to AF-C mode. It follows the movement using AF points, staying focused as long as you keep some points on the subject. The focus only remains fixed if the subject stops moving.

Single AF (AF-S)

Use Single AF mode when your subject isn't moving much, like a building, a group photo, or a scenic view. It's okay for slow-moving subjects, but you must adjust the autofocus as they move.

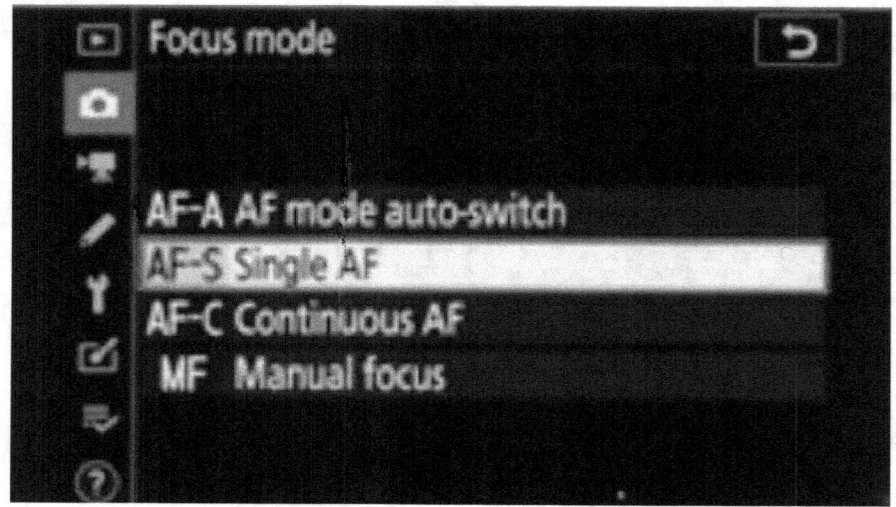

Consider these situations to decide when to use it:

- **The subject is not moving:** When you push the Focus button, the camera quickly focuses on your subject and waits for you to take the picture. If your subject moves and you don't press the Focus button again, the focus won't work well. Take the picture promptly once the focus is set. This mode is great for still subjects or ones that move very slowly.

- **The subject is regularly moving:** The AF-S autofocus mode locks focus on your subject when you press the shutter-release button halfway. However, if the subject moves even slightly after focus is locked, the image may be out of focus. To maintain focus on a moving subject, you need to lift your finger off the shutter-release button and repress it to refocus. This can become tedious, especially if your subject is constantly moving or has erratic movements. In such scenarios, AF-C (continuous autofocus) mode is a more suitable choice. Unlike AF-S, which locks focus, AF-C continuously adjusts focus as your subject moves, keeping it in focus throughout the shooting process. This is particularly useful when photographing moving subjects, such as people, animals, or sports events.

Continuous AF (AF-C)

Continuous AF (AF-C) mode keeps adjusting the focus as long as you hold the Focus button. Even small movements of the camera or the subject make the Z30 camera refocus.

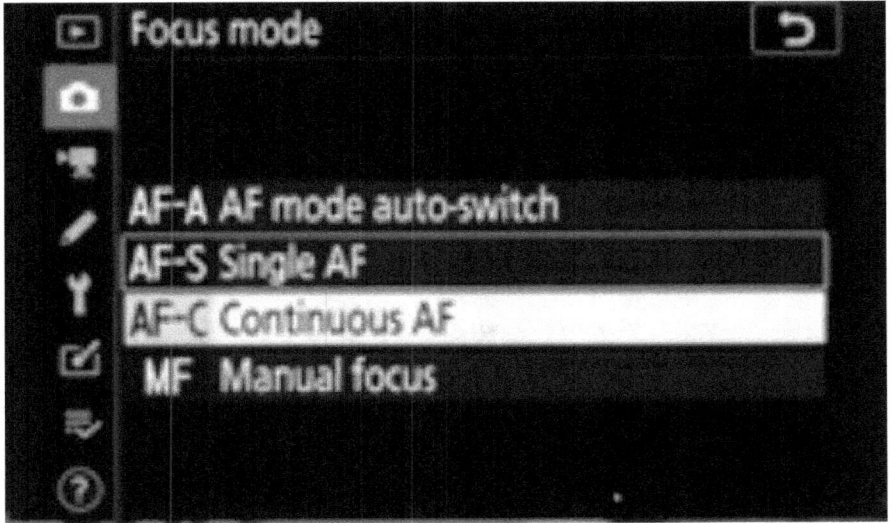

Pay attention to these three situations:

- **The subject is not moving:** When you press and hold the Focus button, and your subject is not moving, Continuous AF works similarly to Single AF, except it doesn't lock the focus. If your camera or subject moves, the autofocus will make small adjustments. Be cautious not to accidentally move the focus point away from your subject, as it might focus on the background instead.
- **The subject is moving across the Viewfinder:** When you press the Focus button and your subject moves around in the camera view, you should keep the focus point on the subject, no matter which focus mode you're using. You can change the size of the focus point, and we'll talk more about that in the next section on AF-Area Modes.
- **The subject is moving toward or away from the camera:** When you press and hold the Focus button, and your subject is moving closer or farther away, the camera has a feature called Predictive Focus Tracking. This feature predicts how much the subject will move right before taking a photo. So, if your subject is moving towards you, the lens adjusts slightly ahead to ensure the picture is sharp when the shutter opens at the perfect moment.

Full-Time AF (AF-F)

The Full-time AF (AF-F) mode is exclusively available in Movie mode, specifically designed to maintain continuous focus on a detected subject without the need for manual intervention. This mode provides constantly updating autofocus, adapting to the chosen AF-area mode. The size and shape of the focus square (AF point) dynamically adjust based on the selected AF-area mode.

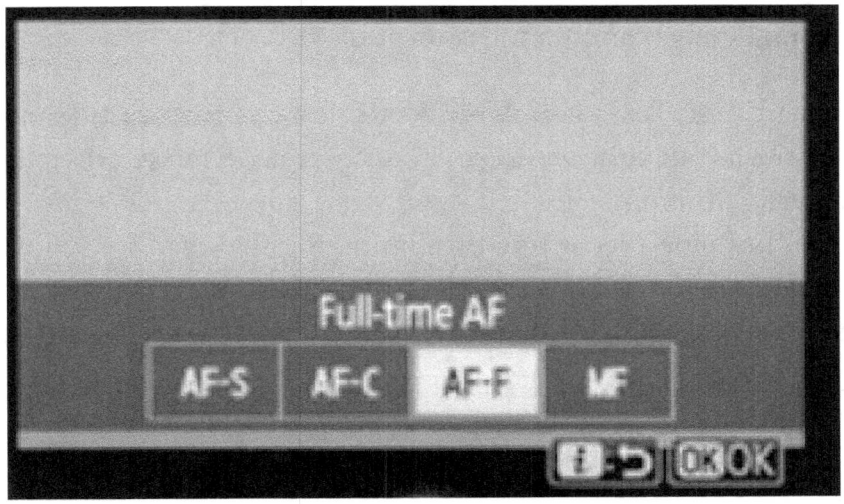

In all AF-area modes, except for Auto-area AF, you'll need to keep the focus square (AF point) on your subject to ensure accurate focus. Many videographers utilize AF-F mode in conjunction with Auto-area AF mode, enabling the camera to not only continuously update focus but also track the subject, keeping it in sharp focus throughout the recording.

When using AF-F Focus mode, the focus doesn't lock onto the subject; instead, it continuously updates unless you press the Focus button. Pressing the Focus button temporarily locks the focus as long as you hold the button down. Upon releasing pressure from the Focus button, the camera unlocks the focus and instantly resumes continuous autofocus.

In essence, the camera behaves as if it's in AF-S mode when the Focus button is pressed and AF-C mode when the button is released. You don't necessarily need to press the Focus button unless you want to force a refocus. The camera will automatically maintain focus on your subject.

Your primary task with AF-F Focus mode is to keep the focus square on your subject, except in Auto-area AF mode, where the camera automatically chooses the subject. AF-F mode simplifies video recording by eliminating the need for manual focus adjustment, allowing you to concentrate on framing and composition while the camera ensures crisp and uninterrupted focus.

Manual Focus (MF)

Manual focus mode lets you control focusing by turning the focus ring on the lens. You can utilize your eyes or other tools to help you focus.

Visible Focus Point

In Manual Focus mode, you have the option to keep the AF point visible in the Viewfinder or turn it off. The AF point, shown between model Lilly Mae's eyes in the image, serves as a visual guide for manual focusing.

When the focus ring is adjusted and the area under the focus point is in sharp focus, the red AF point will turn green. This visual confirmation can be helpful in achieving accurate manual focus.

If you prefer to disable the AF point, the EVF and Monitor will not display any AF points. In this case, you will need to rely entirely on your eyesight or other manual focus assistance tools (which will be discussed shortly) to achieve precise focus.

The choice of whether to display the AF point or not depends on your personal preference and focusing technique. Some photographers find the AF point to be a helpful visual cue, while others prefer the clean and unobstructed view of the scene provided by a hidden AF point.

To turn on or off the onscreen AF point for Manual focus (MF) mode, do these simple steps:

1. Navigate through the Custom Setting Menu > Autofocus > Focus point options > Manual focus mode.
2. On the final screen (image 4), select On to turn on the onscreen AF point or Off to turn it off. It's helpful to keep it on for focusing on a particular area during Manual focus.

Focus Peaking Highlights

Peaking highlights, also known as focus peaking, help find the perfect focus when manually adjusting your camera. This feature adds coloured edges around your subject to clearly show where the focus is best.

If you primarily rely on manual focus, enabling peaking highlights is highly recommended. Here's how to activate this feature:

1. Access the Custom Settings menu.
2. Navigate to the Shooting & Display group.
3. Select d8: Peaking highlights.
4. Choose from the available peaking levels: Low, Standard, and High. Higher peaking levels provide more intense highlighting, making it easier to identify focused areas.
5. Select the desired peaking highlight color: Red, Yellow, White, or Blue. Choose a color that contrasts well with your subject matter.

Once enabled, peaking highlights will appear in the viewfinder and monitor, providing a visual guide for accurate manual focusing. Experiment with different peaking levels and colors to find the combination that best suits your preferences and shooting conditions.

AF-area modes

The AF-area modes help you choose the size of the focus point in your camera. A bigger focus point means a larger subject area is considered for clear focus. To adjust these settings, use the i Menu by pressing the i button or other options mentioned in this section.

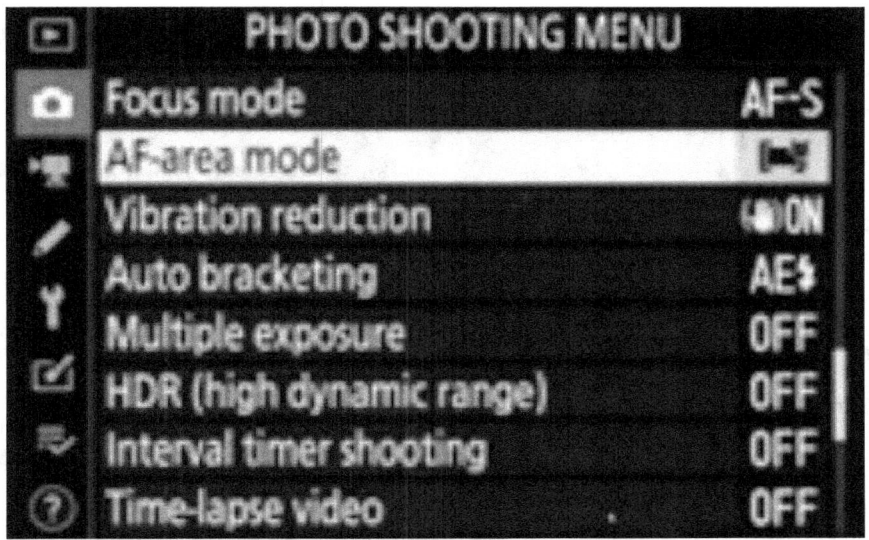

Make sure to choose the right Photo or Movie mode when adjusting settings. The camera has different settings for focusing in Photo and Movie modes.

When using AF-area modes to focus on your subject, you can zoom in close to check the focus and adjust it if needed. Just touch the Zoom In button on the Monitor to zoom in and the Zoom Out button to return.

Let's look at each AF-area mode and discuss what they do.

Pinpoint AF

Pinpoint AF is a highly specialized autofocus mode designed to provide precise focus on a very small area of your subject. This mode allows you to focus with pinpoint accuracy on specific details, such as the pupil of an eye or a water droplet on a leaf.

41

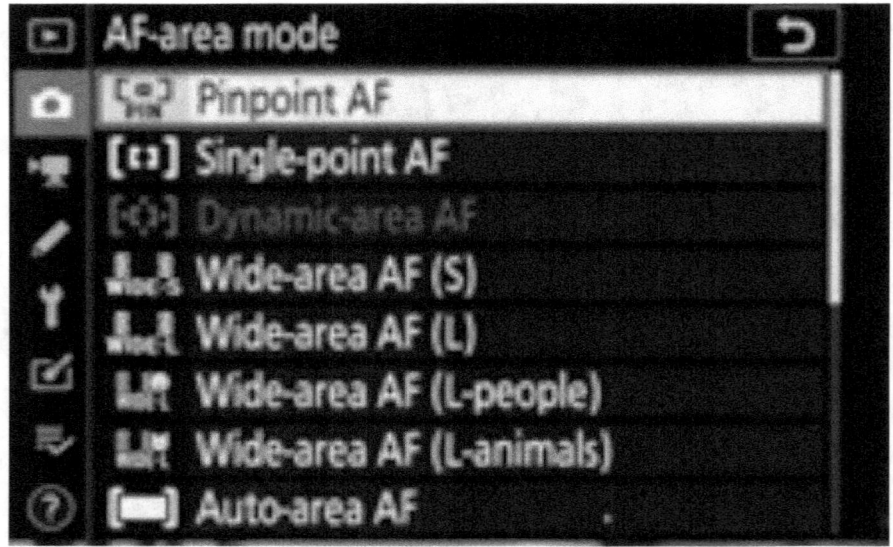

Unlike other autofocus modes that utilize phase-detection autofocus (PDAF), Pinpoint AF relies solely on contrast-detection autofocus (CDAF). While CDAF is generally slower than PDAF, it offers exceptional precision, making it ideal for situations where razor-sharp focus is crucial.

To navigate the Pinpoint AF square within the 209 AF points displayed in the EVF or on the Monitor, simply use the Multi selector pad. Once the camera achieves accurate focus, the Pinpoint AF square will change from red to green, providing a visual confirmation.

It's important to note that Pinpoint AF is only available when Single AF (AF-S) Focus mode is selected. It becomes inactive in Continuous AF (AF-C) Focus mode and is not accessible in Movie mode. This restriction reflects the fact that Pinpoint AF is primarily intended for precise focusing on static subjects rather than continuously tracking moving subjects.

Single-point AF

Single-point AF is a widely preferred autofocus mode among photographers due to its balance of speed and precision. This mode provides a larger AF point frame compared to Pinpoint AF, allowing for more precise focus placement within the 209 AF points distributed across the frame.

Single-point AF strikes a balance between speed and accuracy, outperforming Pinpoint AF in terms of focusing speed while maintaining a high degree of precision. Initially, this mode utilizes phase-detection autofocus (PDAF) for rapid focus acquisition. According to Nikon, Single-point AF then employs contrast-detection autofocus (CDAF) as a final step to verify and refine focus accuracy.

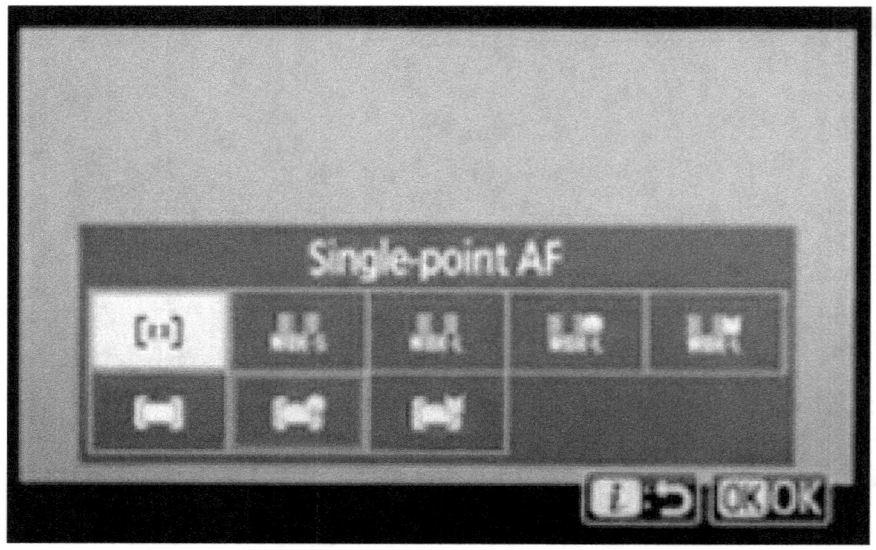

To navigate the Single-point AF square within the EVF or on the Monitor, you can either use the Multi selector pad or directly touch your subject on the Monitor. When the camera achieves accurate focus, the AF point square will change from red to green, provided you are using Single AF (AF-S) Focus mode. In Continuous AF (AF-C) Focus mode, the AF square remains red as the camera continuously seeks active focus.

Single-point AF AF-area mode offers versatility in its compatibility with both AF-S and AF-C Focus modes. Additionally, it can be employed in both Photo and Movie modes, making it a versatile tool for various shooting scenarios. Whether you're capturing still images or recording videos, Single-point AF provides precise focus control, ensuring that your subject remains in sharp focus.

Dynamic-area AF

Dynamic-area AF is an intelligent autofocus mode designed to effectively track moving subjects while maintaining focus accuracy. You can see the center Dynamic-area AF point square, surrounded by additional active AF points, positioned on model Lilly Mae's left eye. Unlike Single-point AF, which utilizes a single active AF point, Dynamic-area AF employs a group of nine AF points, including the center point.

This configuration enables the camera to continuously monitor the surrounding area around the primary focus point, ensuring that if the subject moves or the camera position changes, another active AF point can seamlessly take over focus tracking.

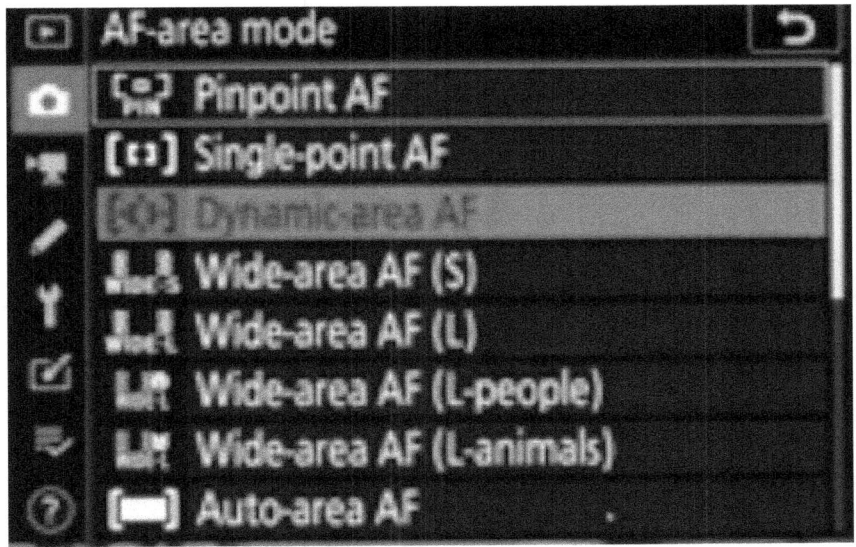

Dynamic-area AF continuously seeks focus, keeping all AF points within the red AF point frame actively engaged. The color of the frame remains red, regardless of focus acquisition, as this mode prioritizes continuous focus tracking over visual confirmation.

To navigate the Dynamic-area AF frame within the EVF or on the Monitor, you can either use the Multi selector pad or directly touch your subject on the Monitor. This mode is available for Photo mode only, making it an ideal choice for capturing moving subjects in still images. However, it is not accessible in Movie mode due to the continuous focus adjustments required for video recording.

Dynamic-area AF is compatible solely with Continuous AF (AF-C) Focus mode. When Single AF (AF-S) Focus mode is selected, Dynamic-area AF becomes inactive and grayed out on the Photo Shooting Menu and i Menu. This restriction reflects the fact that Dynamic-area AF is specifically designed to track moving subjects, a capability that is more relevant in Continuous AF mode.

Wide-area AF (S)

The Wide-area AF (S) mode is like Single-point AF but with more focus points in a wider frame. The red frame is much bigger than the Single-point AF frame, and all its hidden focus points work.

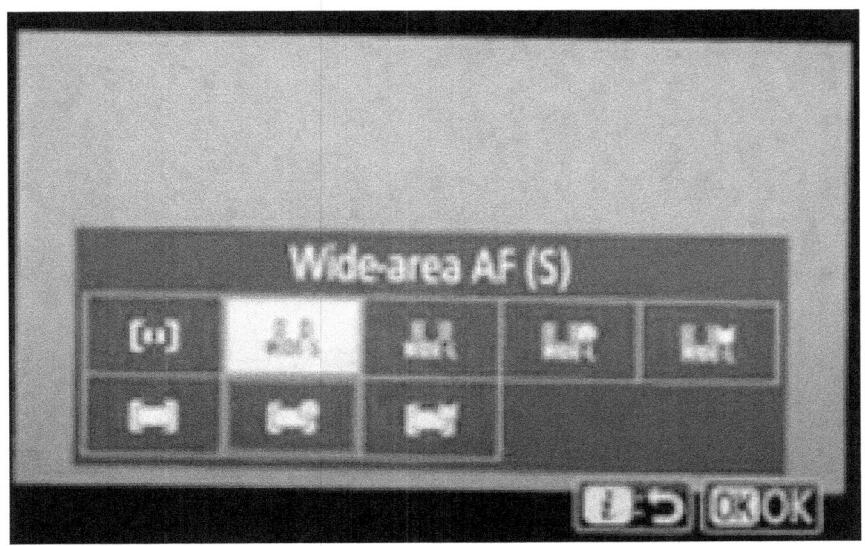

Moving the focus frame around using the Multi-selector pad or touching your subject on the Monitor. In Single AF (AF-S) mode, the frame turns green when focused, while in Continuous AF (AF-C) mode, it stays red as the camera keeps seeking focus. Wide-area AF (S) works in both AF-S and AF-C modes and in Photo and Movie modes.

Wide-area AF (L)

Moving the focus frame around using the Multi-selector pad or touching your subject on the Monitor. In Single AF (AF-S) mode, the frame turns green when focused, while in Continuous AF (AF-C) mode, it stays red as the camera keeps seeking focus. Wide-area AF (S) works in both AF-S and AF-C modes and in Photo and Movie modes.

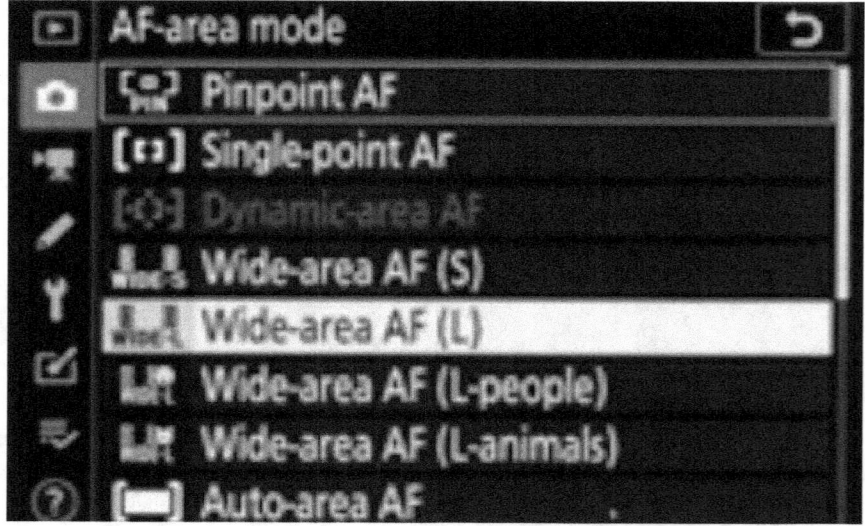

You can move the focus point on the screen using the arrows or by touching the subject. When the camera focuses well, the frame turns green in Single AF mode but stays red in Continuous AF mode because it keeps seeking focus.

You can use the Wide-area AF (L) mode for focusing in both AF-S and AF-C modes, and it works in both Photo and Movie modes, too.

Wide-area AF (L-People)

Wide-area AF (L-People) is an AF-area mode on Nikon Z30 cameras that is specifically designed to focus on human faces and eyes. This mode is a good option for portraits and other situations where you want to make sure that your subject's face is in focus.

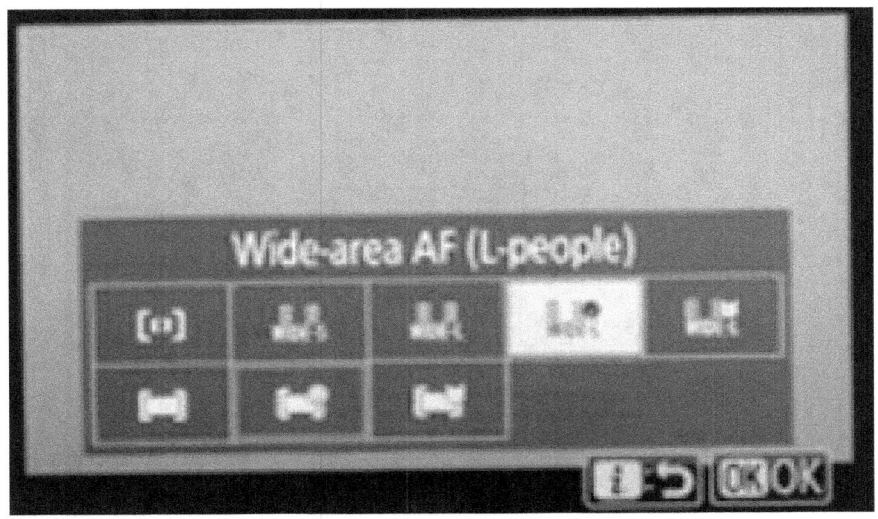

When Wide-area AF (L-People) is selected, the camera uses a wide area of the frame to detect and focus on human faces and eyes. This means that you don't need to worry about manually selecting a focus point, and the camera will keep your subject's face in focus even if they move around a little.

Auto-area AF

Auto-area AF lets the camera decide where to focus without your input. It usually picks the nearest and brightest object in the frame.

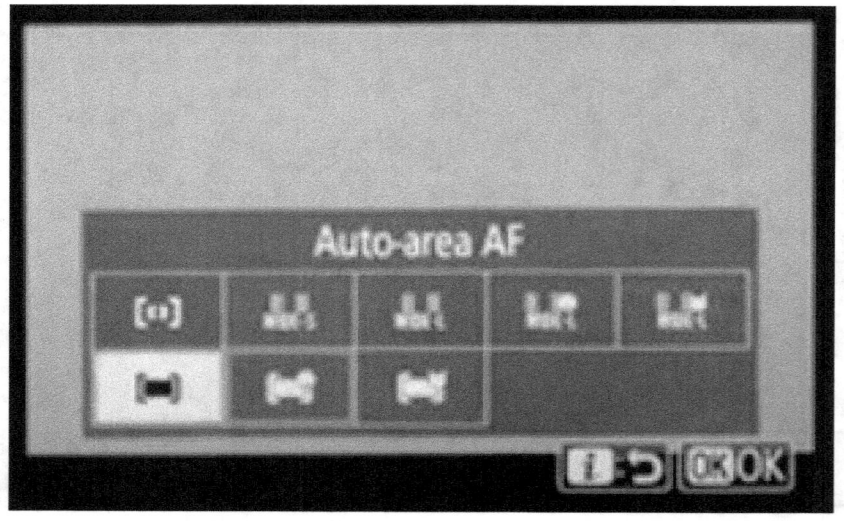

Sometimes, the camera might be tricked if the background has high contrast. Nikon updates the firmware to enhance autofocus, and the Z30 performs well with Auto-area AF, which is a bit more complicated than other focus modes.

Auto-area AF (People)

The Auto-area AF (People) setting on the Nikon Z30 is designed to automatically detect and focus on human faces or eyes. This can be a helpful feature for portraits, snapshots, and other situations where you want to make sure that your subject's face is in focus.

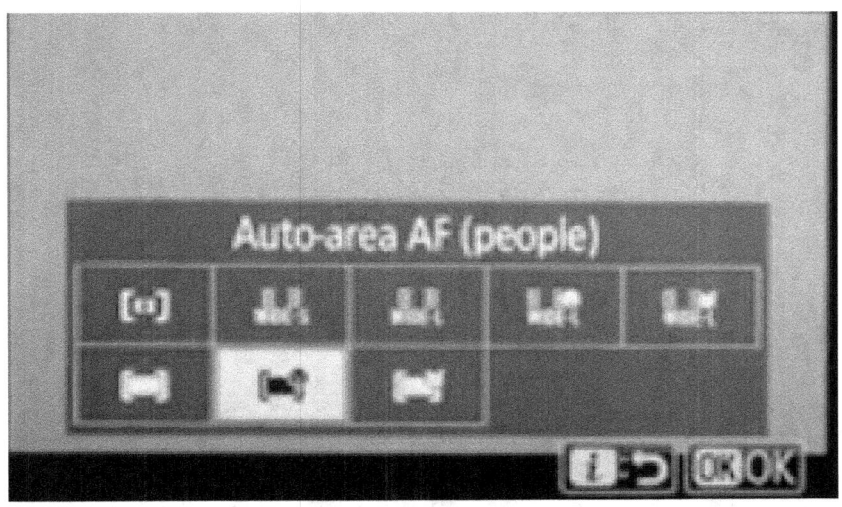

To use Auto-area AF (People), simply select it as your AF-area mode. The camera will then automatically detect any human faces or eyes in the frame and focus on them. If there are multiple faces or eyes in the frame, the camera will prioritize the closest one to the center of the frame.

Auto-area AF (Animal)

The Auto-area AF (Animal) setting on the Nikon Z30 is a handy feature that lets the camera automatically detect and focus on the faces and eyes of dogs and cats. When the camera detects the face of a dog or cat, a focus point (yellow border) will be displayed around the subject's face or, if the camera detects eyes, over one or the other of its eyes. This can be a helpful feature for pet portraits, snapshots, and other situations where you want to make sure that your furry friend is in focus.

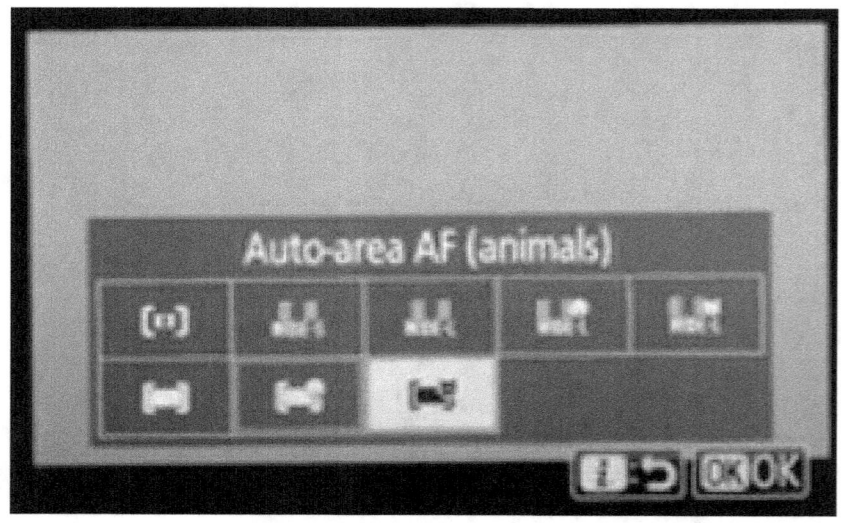

CHAPTER 3: MASTERING COLOR CONTROLS

Understanding the White Balance Setting

Usually, White balance (WB) helps ensure whites look white and other colors are right in different lighting. You can also use it to add cool color effects to your pictures.

The camera's white balance temperature scale works differently from the Kelvin scale we learn about for star temperatures. Unlike stars, where red giants are cool and blue/white stars are hot, white balance adds color to compensate for a lack of color in the original light instead of following the temperature-based color emission of a "blackbody."

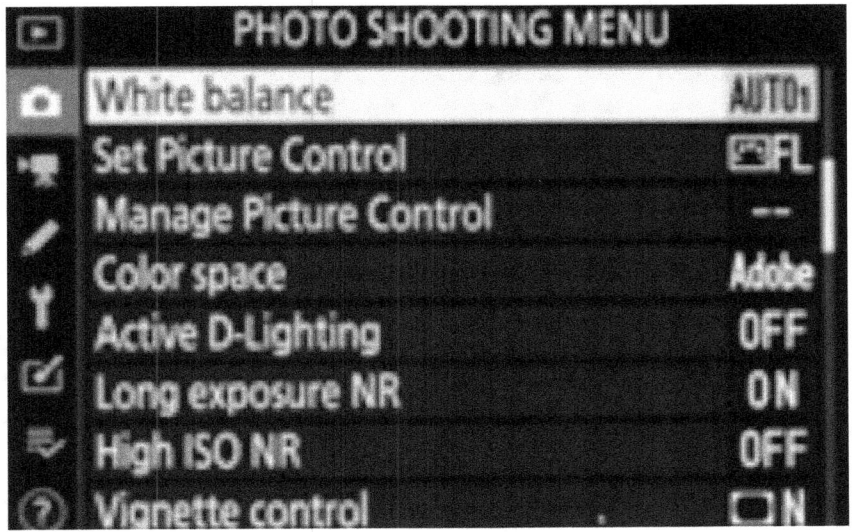

Fluorescent lights lack blue, making things look greenish yellow. The camera adds blue to even it out, making the colors look normal. The white balance for most fluorescent lights is about 4000K.

Imagine taking a picture on a cloudy day. If you don't do anything, the picture looks bluish because of the cool light. Your camera's White balance control detects this and adds red to warm the colors. So, the White balance could be around 6000K on a cloudy day.

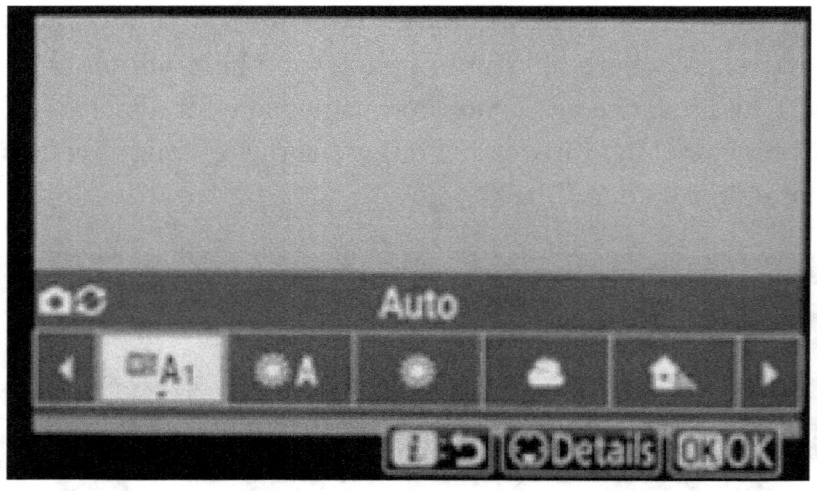

Regarding temperature in photography, red colors are warm, and blue colors are cool. It's different from what we learn in school, but for photographers, blue feels cool, and red feels warm. Don't let your astronomer friends tell you otherwise.

Grasping white balance (WB) means recognizing that light comes in different colors, ranging from cool to warm. Adjusting our cameras correctly helps capture accurate and balanced colors, compensating for the actual light source. The image may have a color cast if we don't balance the settings. This chapter explores how the Z30 camera controls handle white balance.

Adjusting the White Balance setting

The Nikon Z30 has three ways to adjust its white balance. Now, let's talk about each method.

WB on the i Menu

To adjust the color balance, press the i button and choose White Balance in the menu. Ensure the Photo/Video switch is set right for your actions—photos or videos can have different color settings.

WB on the Photo and Movie Shooting Menus

The WB settings in the Photo Shooting Menu impact photos, and the ones in the Movie Shooting Menu affect videos. Despite a small distinction we'll cover, both menus operate similarly. You can use different WB settings for photos and videos.

Assigning White balance to a camera button

If you often adjust the White balance on your camera, you can set it to a quick button like Fn1 or Fn2. To change White balance for photos, use still image mode; for videos, use Movie mode. Now, let's look at each way to adjust White balance.

WB on the i Menu

White Balance on the i Menu

Most photographers and videographers prefer using the Z30's i Menu to pick the right White Balance because it's easily accessible. Now, let's see how to use the i Menu to select White Balance.

To set the White balance on your camera, follow these easy steps:

1. Press the "i" button with your subject on the screen.
2. Choose White balance, pick a setting (like Direct sunlight), and press OK.
3. For more control, fine-tune the colors using the arrows or tapping Adjust, and lock it in by pressing OK when satisfied.

Auto White Balance on the i Menu

The Auto White Balance setting lets you pick and adjust one of three options (A0, A1, or A2) on a special screen. We'll check it out using the i Menu with the lens cap to make the screen contrast as high as possible.

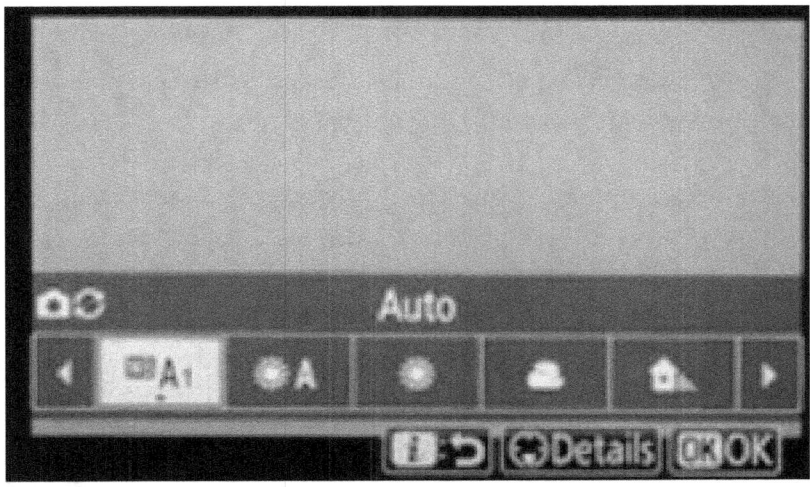

To adjust the white balance on your camera, follow these simple steps:

1. Press the "i" button with your subject on the screen to open the menu. Select White Balance on the bottom row, first position on the left, and press OK.
2. Scroll to Auto WB on the left, and press OK to lock the current setting (like A1). To change, use the Multi-selector or tap Details.
3. Choose one of the three Auto WB values: A0 (reduce warm colors), A1 (keep overall atmosphere), or A2 (keep warm lighting colors). To fine-tune, highlight the value and press down on the Multi-selector or tap Adjust.
4. Fine-tune using four color axes: green (G), amber (A), magenta (M), and blue (B). Move the black square towards or between axes to see color changes. Once satisfied, press OK to lock it in.

57

Fluorescent White Balance on the i Menu

The Fluorescent WB setting lets you pick and adjust one of seven fluorescent types using an extra screen.

Follow these steps to adjust the Fluorescent White Balance on your camera:

1. Press the "i" button with your subject on the screen to open the menu. Select White Balance from the bottom row, first position on the left, and press OK or tap the WB position.
2. Find Fluorescent WB and press OK (e.g., 4) to lock the current setting. To choose a different setting, scroll down or tap Details.
3. Choose one of the seven Fluorescent WB values: Sodium-vapor lamps (1), Warm-white fluorescent (2), White fluorescent (3), Cool-white fluorescent (4), Day white fluorescent (5), Daylight fluorescent (6), or High temp. Mercury-vapor (7). To fine-tune, highlight the value and press down on the Multi-selector pad or tap Adjust.
4. Fine-tune using four color axes: green (G), amber (A), magenta (M), and blue (B). Move the black square towards or between axes, observing the color change. Press OK when satisfied to lock it in.

K White Balance on the i Menu

The K WB setting has a special screen where you can pick and adjust a particular color temperature from 2500K to 10000K.

To set or adjust the White balance on your camera, follow these simple steps:

1. Press the "i" button with your subject on the screen, go to White Balance, and select the first option on the left.
2. Choose the K WB item, lock in the default (5000K) setting, or pick a different value. Use the up/down buttons to adjust within 2500K to 10000K.
3. Make adjustments for three settings by tapping the up/down pointers. Press OK to lock in the chosen K WB value.
4. Fine-tune the color by moving the yellow box to the right. Use the Multi-selector pad or touch pointers to add magenta (down) or green (up). No adjustments for blue or amber are allowed. Press OK when satisfied with the fine-tuning.

PRE White Balance on the i Menu

The PRE WB setting helps you make and save white balance settings on your camera. You can choose from existing settings or make your own. The camera reads a white or gray card in the current lighting to create these settings.

To set or make a custom white balance on your camera:

1. Aim your camera at a well-lit white or gray card; don't worry about focus, and press the 'i' button. Select White Balance from the menu.
2. Select the PRE White Balance option (like PRE1), press OK to lock the current setting, or scroll down to measure a new one.

3. Pick a memory slot (d-1 to d-6) where you want to save the measurement. Press OK to confirm.

4. On the main menu, tap on OK–Measure mode. It activates the measurement screen.

5. The chosen PRE number will flash. Bring the white or gray card close to the lens, avoiding shadows. Press OK to measure. The camera will capture the ambient light for that custom white balance setting.

6. You'll see a screen if the white balance reading works. The camera will say "Data acquired," and the reading is saved in the memory location you picked (d–1 to d–6). Now, you can take accurate pictures under the current light. If the reading doesn't work, the camera will say, "Unable to measure white balance. Please try again." It might happen if it's too dark, the card reflects too much light, or there's a shadow. If it fails, move the camera or change cards and try again.

WB on the Photo and Movie Shooting Menus

Choose the right White Balance by going to the Photo Shooting Menu or Movie Shooting Menu. I'll explain using the Photo Shooting Menu as an example, but the Movie Shooting Menu works similarly, with a few small differences that we'll review.

To set the White balance on your camera, follow these steps:

1. Go to the White balance option in the Photo or Movie Shooting Menu.

2. Choose a White balance value like "Direct sunlight" and press OK to confirm. Note that slight differences exist between the Photo and Movie menus, like the absence of Flash WB in Movie mode.

3. If you want to adjust the White balance further, highlight a value, scroll right, or tap on Adjust. You can fine-tune Auto WB using the green (G), amber (A), magenta (M), and blue (B) axes. Move the black square to adjust the color, then press OK when satisfied.

Auto White Balance on the Photo/Movie Shooting Menus

The Auto White Balance setting has a screen where you can pick and adjust one of three Auto White Balance options (AUTO0, AUTO1, or AUTO2).

Here's how to adjust the white balance on your camera in simpler terms:

1. Go to the White Balance option in your camera's menu.
2. Pick Auto WB (like AUTO1) and press OK. If you want a different Auto WB, scroll right.
3. Choose AUTO0 for less warm colors, AUTO1 for the overall atmosphere, or AUTO2 for warm lighting. If you want to tweak it, highlight your choice and move right on the selector pad or tap Adjust.
4. For fine-tuning, use four color axes: green, amber, magenta, and blue. Move the black square toward these axes until you're happy, then press OK to save your adjustments.

Fluorescent White Balance on the Photo/Movie Shooting Menus

The Fluorescent WB setting provides an additional screen for selecting and fine-tuning one of the seven available fluorescent types. This allows you to achieve more precise white balance compensation under various fluorescent lighting conditions.

To choose and/or fine-tune a Fluorescent WB type, follow these steps:

1. Access the White Balance option from either the Photo or Movie Shooting Menu.
2. Scroll to the Fluorescent WB item (e.g., 4) and press or touch the OK button to confirm the current Fluorescent WB setting. To change to a different Fluorescent WB setting, use the Multi selector pad to scroll to the right. The next screen will present you with the seven available WB values.
3. Select one of the seven Fluorescent WB types and press or touch the OK button to confirm your choice. If you want to fine-tune the white balance color setting, highlight one of the Fluorescent WB values and scroll to the right with the Multi selector pad or tap on the "Adjust" option.
4. To fine-tune the current Fluorescent WB, you can adjust four color axes: green (G), amber (A), magenta (M), and blue (B). Move the small black square towards any of the axes or between two of them. Once you are satisfied with the fine-tuning, press or touch the OK button to confirm your adjustments.

K White Balance on the Photo/Movie Shooting Menus

Using an extra screen, the K WB setting lets you pick and adjust a particular color warmth between 2500K and 10000K.

To set or adjust the white balance on your camera:

1. Go to the Photo or Movie Shooting Menu and select White Balance.
2. Find the "K Choose color temperature" option to confirm with OK. The default is 5000K, but you can change it by scrolling on the selector pad.
3. The screen will show a range from 2500K to 10000K. Adjust the three settings using the up/down pointers or selector pad, then press OK.
4. For fine-tuning, move the yellow box to the right. Press down for magenta and up for green. No adjustments for blue or amber. Once satisfied, press OK to confirm.

PRE White Balance on the Photo/Movie Shooting Menu

The PRE (Preset Manual) WB setting lets you save specific white balance readings for different lighting conditions. You can name and protect these saved values, determined by reading a white or gray card under the current lighting.

You can also choose a photo to set as a white balance reference, copying the white balance from that image to a saved PRE memory location. This way, you can use it when creating new photos and videos.

Let's look at the different options within the PRE WB setting.

Choosing an Existing PRE-White Balance

Setting the white balance using the PRE WB method in the Photo/Movie Shooting Menus can be complex.

1. Go to the White Balance option in the Photo or Movie Shooting Menu.
2. Find the Preset manual item (like PRE1).

3. Choose one of the stored white balance settings (d–1 to d–6) and confirm it by pressing OK.

Now, let's look at how to make small adjustments to a Preset manual white balance setting.

Fine-Tuning an Existing PRE-White Balance

Before, we learned how to adjust your camera using a white or gray card and pick a preset white balance. Now, let's find out how to make small adjustments to one of the preset options (d–1 to d–6) before using it.

1. Go to White Balance and select Preset Manual on the third screen.
2. Tap on a memory location or use the Multi-selector to choose one (d–1 to d–6).
3. Press Zoom in or tap Select (not OK) to open the Preset manual menu.
4. Choose Fine-tune, then adjust the color balance with the Multi-selector or by tapping the arrows in the color box.
5. Press OK to save. When you return, you'll see "PRE*" next to White balance, indicating fine-tuned.

Color Temperature

The camera's white balance can go from cool (2500K) to warm (10,000K). The center image looks good; the left is cooler (bluish), and the right is warmer (reddish). In astronomy, the camera white balance is opposite to the star color temperature.

You can now adjust your Z30 camera's colors just like we used to with film and filters. Pick the Cloudy White balance setting at 6000K to get warm, daylight-like photos. For even warmer tones, go for Shade at 8000K. Or let AUTO2 (A2) automatically warm colors based on the light around you.

To give your image a cool or bluish look, choose Cool-white fluorescent (4200K) or Incandescent (3000K) settings when taking pictures in normal daylight. The Z30 camera lets you adjust color temperature from very cool or bluish (2500K) to very warm or reddish (10,000K) without needing different film or filters. It's easy to control color temperature with the camera's settings, and you can pick any value in between. The WB symbols, official names, kelvin values, and specifications are listed in the camera's order.

Auto (3500K to 8000K): This setting has three options: AUTO0 makes whites less warm, AUTO1 keeps colors normal, and AUTO2 makes images a bit warmer, especially with certain lenses like G, E, D, or S Nikkor.

Natural light auto (4500K to 8000K): This setting, like AUTO1 Normal, tweaks the colors in your photos to look more like what you see without a camera. But Natural Light Auto does this in a way better suited for outdoor scenes, like landscapes. If you enjoy taking pictures of nature, give this mode a try.

Direct sunlight (5200K): Use this mode when taking pictures in bright sunlight.

Cloudy (6000K): This setting helps make a picture look warmer when the weather is cloudy.

Shade (8000K): This setting helps reduce the bluish color caused by a sunny sky when you're taking a picture of something in the shadow.

Incandescent (3000K): This setting helps the camera show accurate colors when using an old-style incandescent light bulb as the main light source.

Fluorescent (2700K to 7200K): This setting has seven types of light, like sodium-vapor (2700K), warm-white fluorescent (3000K), white fluorescent (3700K), cool-white fluorescent (4200K), Day white fluorescent (5000K), daylight fluorescent (6500K), and high temp. Mercury-vapor (7200K). Check the bulb's label or packaging to find the right one.

Flash (5400K): Use this setting when you want the color of your Nikon Speedlight to match and stay the same in all your pictures

K (2500K–10,000K): Choose a color from various options to perfectly match the lighting on a subject, especially for important tasks.

PRE (Preset manual): To get the right colors in a photo, we measure the light around using a white or gray card. The camera remembers this measurement (d–1 to d–6) so you can use it again in similar lighting later.

CHAPTER 4: TAKING CHARGE OF EXPOSURE

Introducing the Exposure Trio: Aperture, Shutter Speed, and ISO

Aperture

Aperture priority mode, denoted as "A" on the camera mode dial, provides direct control over the aperture, the opening in the lens that regulates the amount of light entering the camera sensor. This mode allows you to manipulate the aperture to achieve specific photographic effects.

In low-light conditions, increasing the aperture size allows more light to enter the camera, brightening the image. Conversely, in well-lit situations, reducing the aperture size restricts light entry, preventing overexposure.

Beyond its light-control function, aperture also plays a crucial role in depth of field, the range of distance in which objects appear sharp in an image. A large aperture, indicated by a low f-number (e.g., f/1.4, f/2.8), creates a shallow depth of field, blurring the background and emphasizing the foreground subject. This technique is commonly used in portraiture to isolate the subject from the surroundings.

On the other hand, a small aperture, indicated by a high f-number (e.g., f/16, f/22), produces a deep depth of field, keeping both the foreground and background in sharp focus. This approach is often employed in landscape photography to capture the sharpness and detail throughout the scene.

In aperture priority mode, the camera automatically selects the shutter speed based on the chosen aperture value and the available light conditions. This allows you to focus on controlling the aperture to achieve the desired depth of field effect while the camera handles the appropriate shutter speed for correct exposure.

Shutter speed

Shutter speed priority mode, designated as "S" on the camera mode dial, provides direct control over the shutter speed, the duration for which the shutter remains open, exposing the camera sensor to light. This mode allows you to manipulate the shutter speed to capture motion or achieve specific exposure effects.

Fast shutter speeds, measured in fractions of a second (e.g., 1/1000s, 1/500s), are ideal for freezing motion, capturing crisp images of moving subjects, such as athletes, wildlife, or splashing water droplets. By using a fast shutter speed, you can effectively stop motion in its tracks, creating a sense of dynamism and energy in your images.

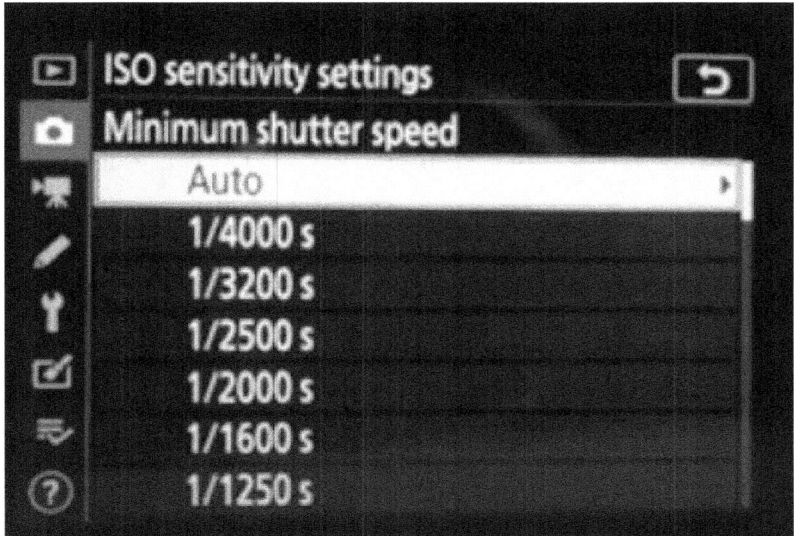

Slower shutter speeds, measured in seconds (e.g., 1s, 2s), are useful for conveying a sense of movement or blurring objects in motion. For instance, slow shutter speeds can be employed to create intentional motion blur, capturing the trails of moving lights or the smooth flow of water. This technique adds a sense of motion and depth to your images.

In shutter speed priority mode, the camera automatically selects the aperture value based on the chosen shutter speed and the available light conditions. This allows you to focus on controlling the shutter speed to achieve the desired motion or exposure effect while the camera handles the appropriate aperture for correct exposure.

ISO sensitivity

In earlier chapters, we touched on ISO. Now, let's explore it more. We'll discuss ISO sensitivity control, how to turn it on/off, adjust sensitivity, and understand the effects of these settings.

Auto ISO sensitivity control

There's a button at the camera's top for ISO. When you press it, the ISO lights up at the bottom, showing the ISO value. It helps you check if it's set to Auto ISO.

How to activate/deactivate Auto ISO control

To switch from Auto mode, press and hold the ISO button. While holding it, turn the dial on the front of the camera. This action disables auto ISO. To re-enable it, repeat the process, and you'll see "Auto" appear below the ISO setting.

Adjusting the ISO Sensitivity

If your camera is set to manual ISO, like ISO 1600, you can change it by holding the ISO button and turning the dial. In Auto mode, the camera picks the ISO, but in the manual, you have control. Hold the ISO button and turn the front control wheel to switch back to auto. If your native ISO is 800 and flashes, auto ISO is higher; set native ISO to 1,000 to stop the flashing. It is unique to this camera.

Exposure compensation

The Exposure Compensation button is located on the top of the camera. When you press this button, you'll notice the ISO value change and a small exposure icon appear. To adjust the exposure compensation, hold down the Exposure Compensation button while rotating the command dial. This allows you to increase or decrease the exposure to fine-tune the brightness of your images.

Exposure compensation is a valuable tool for protecting highlights and unleashing creative possibilities in your photography. By slightly underexposing the image, you can preserve the details in the highlights, which can be challenging to recover if they're blown out. Underexposing slightly can then be compensated for during post-processing, providing more control over the final image.

To assess whether your exposure is capturing the full range of tones, utilize the histogram. Access the histogram by pressing the Display button. The histogram displays the distribution of light and dark tones in your image, with brighter tones on the left. If the histogram bunches up towards the right edge, it indicates that some highlights are overexposed and may be lost. By adjusting the exposure compensation, you can ensure that the histogram covers the entire range, preserving both highlights and shadows.

Exposure compensation empowers you to take control of your exposure, allowing you to protect highlights, enhance creativity, and capture images that reflect your artistic vision.

Exploring the Histogram

As you adjust the exposure compensation, observe how the histogram changes. The marks on the histogram shift to the right as the image gets brighter, indicating an increase in exposure. Conversely, turning the dial to the left darkens the image, and the marks on the histogram shift to the left. This visual representation helps you understand how exposure compensation affects the distribution of tones in your image.

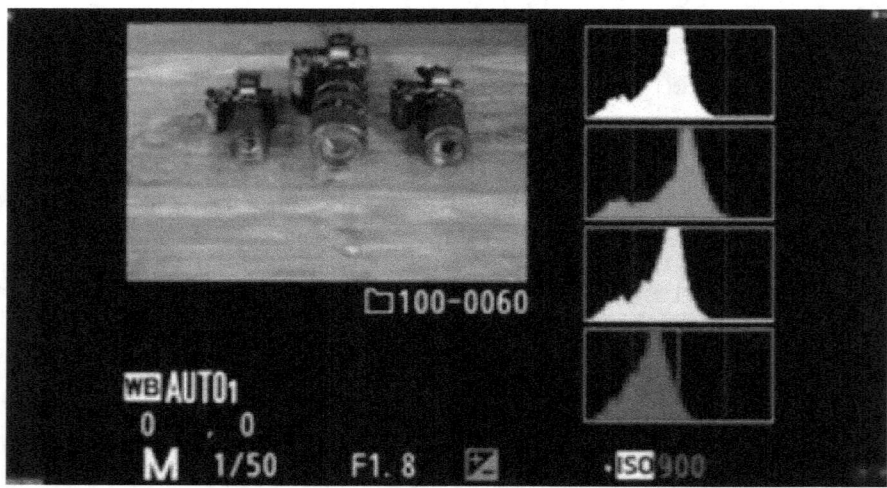

You can keep the histogram displayed while shooting to monitor the camera's exposure metering. If the histogram shows a well-balanced distribution of tones, with shadows, highlights, and midtones represented, the camera is doing a good job of exposing the scene. However, if the scene has a bright object that causes the histogram to bunch up on the right side, indicating overexposed highlights, you may need to use exposure compensation to adjust the overall brightness and preserve the details in the highlights. In such cases, the histogram serves as a valuable tool for making informed exposure decisions.

Utilizing the AF-L/AE-L Button for Auto Exposure Lock

The AF-L/AE-L button, located on the front of the camera, serves a dual purpose: autofocusing and auto exposure lock. When pressed, it locks the focus and exposure settings, preventing them from changing even if the scene or subject conditions alter. This feature is particularly useful in situations where you want to maintain a specific focus point and exposure while recomposing the shot.

For instance, if you're photographing a portrait with a bright background, you can press the AF-L/AE-L button while focusing on the subject's eyes to ensure that the focus remains locked. Then, you can recompose the shot to include more of the background without worrying about the camera automatically refocusing or adjusting the exposure.

The AF-L/AE-L button provides a convenient way to maintain control over both focus and exposure, allowing you to capture the desired composition without compromising focus accuracy or exposure settings.

Stepping Up to Advanced Exposure Modes (P, Tv, Av, and M)

You can find a few more settings when you're in the i menu. There's Auto dynamic-range lighting metering (which we discussed before), and changing it can affect your photo's brightness. Highlight priority makes it darker to protect highlights, Spot metering focuses on where you aim, Center-weight average uses the center for brightness, and Matrix mode considers the whole screen. These are helpful tools for getting the right exposure in different situations, and we'll explore them more in this chapter.

Program-Auto mode

Let's explore some additional features using Program-auto mode (P mode). In this mode, you can adjust the ISO settings. Program-auto mode provides more options; for instance, in the menu, you can access various previously unavailable settings in Auto mode.

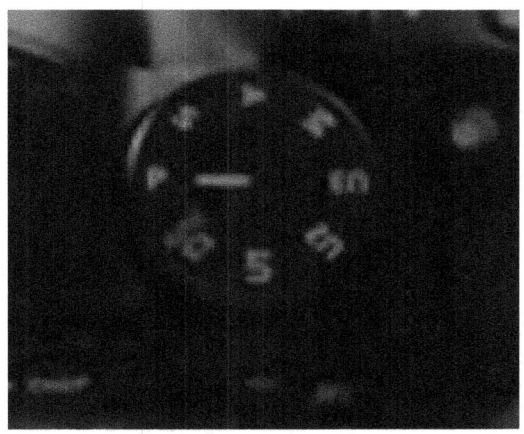

Program Auto- video mode

In Program Auto mode, which provides more control over camera settings compared to fully automatic modes, ISO remains locked and cannot be manually adjusted. This restriction applies even when you're in video mode. To manually control ISO while recording video, you'll need to switch to the full-fledged manual mode. Remember this if you're accustomed to having ISO readily accessible in other modes and want to adjust it during video recording.

When recording videos, it's recommended to use the Position Focus point instead of Touch AF. Touch AF can cause abrupt focus changes that appear jarring and unnatural in video footage. Instead, the Position Focus point provides a smoother, more controlled focus transition, ensuring that your subject remains in sharp focus throughout the recording.

To switch between Touch AF and Position Focus point, simply tap on the AF-area mode icon on the screen. Select "Position

Focus point" for smoother focus transitions during video recording.

Shutter Priority Mode

Let's set the camera to Shutter priority mode (S). Make sure you're in Photo mode. When you turn the dial, you'll see the shutter speed change. Turn it one way to make it slower, from 1/13th to 1/15th of a second.

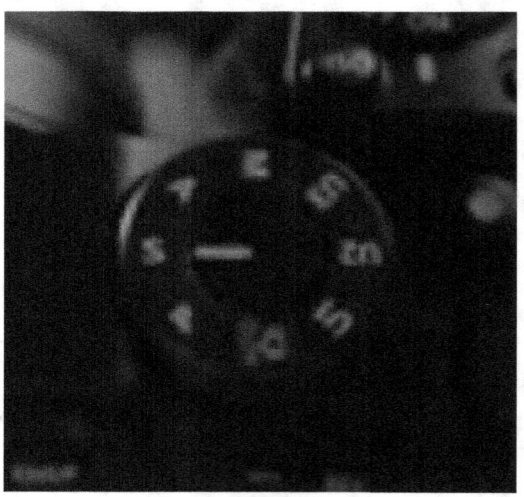

Motion Blur

The F number is like the eye's pupil size, changing when the number changes. It's called Aperture. Imagine it's your eye. Shutter speed is like a clock; 1/15th second is slow, making motion blurry in photos. Slower, like 1/8th, makes it super blurry – that's Motion blur. Use Shutter priority mode for that.

If you want a slow shutter for cool effects like blurry water or streaky lights, use it when capturing motion. For example, if you're tracking a car and want a blurred background (called Panning), use a slower shutter speed. Shutter priority is also for freezing action, like in sports. Adjust the shutter speed to around 1/500th of a second for fast-moving subjects. You can use Auto ISO, but manually setting it can be handy. Just hold down the ISO button, turn the dial, and aim for a non-blinking F to ensure proper exposure, usually around ISO 4500.

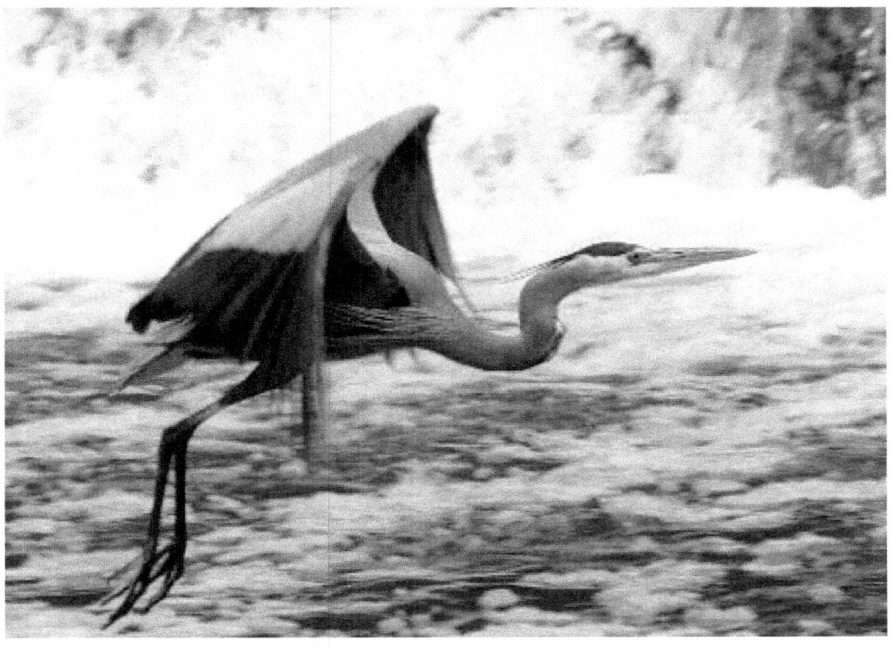

If you turn off auto ISO, your camera blinks to warn you of improper exposure. Without fixing it, your photo will be black due to low sensitivity. Auto ISO at 4000 ensures good exposure, especially for fast-moving subjects like athletes, resulting in a frozen action when you check the playback. It is thanks to the fast shutter speed in Shutter priority mode.

Aperture priority mode

Let's talk about the Aperture priority mode, also known as the A mode. Instead of the shutter, you'll notice a box around the Aperture. A number like F 3.8 indicates the Aperture. By turning the camera's front dial, you change this number, adjusting the size of the lens opening.

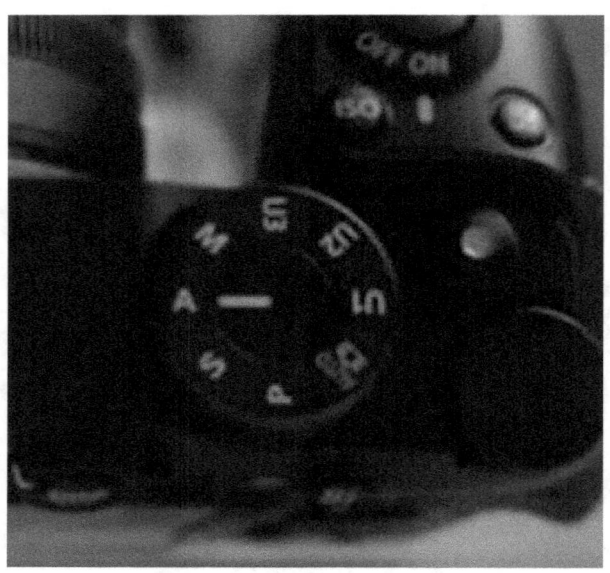

Now, the Aperture also affects something called depth of field. The background becomes blurry when you focus on a specific area, like a face. So, when you focus on a person's face in this mode, the background gets pleasantly blurry.

Depth of field is like a slice of focus in a photo. When you focus on something, the depth of field is how much in front and behind it stays sharp. If you use a low F number, the focus slice is thin, blurting the background. A higher F number, like F16, makes more things sharp around the focus point. So, a small F number for a blurry background and a big F number for a clear background.

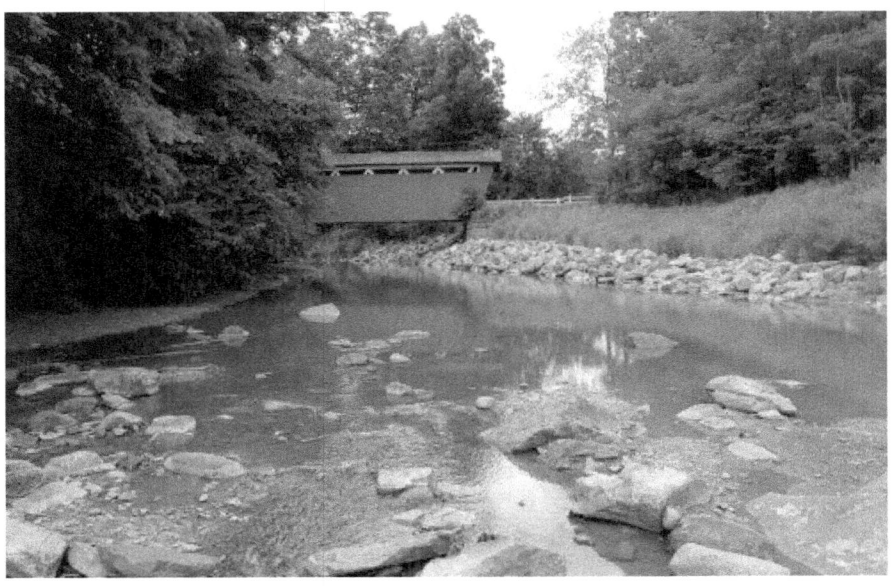

For pictures of people, use a lower aperture number to blur the background. Imagine taking a portrait – a low aperture like F 6.3 will give you a super blurry background when you zoom in. Check it in the Playback menu, and you'll see the face is sharp, but the background is completely blurred. If you use a higher aperture like F16 or F22, the background is still blurry, but you can see more details. So, F16 gives a clearer background compared to the more blurred F6.3.

Minimum Shutter

In aperture priority mode, the minimum shutter speed is another thing to understand. When using auto ISO, the camera picks the shutter speed. If, for instance, it's set at 1/30th of a second and you're capturing active subjects like kids in a portrait, you might want a faster shutter speed to avoid blurriness.

To capture fast-moving scenes:

1. Adjust your camera settings.
2. In aperture priority mode, go to the menu, find ISO sensitivity settings under Photo Shooting Menu, and select Minimum shutter speed.
3. Choose Auto for a preferable option, or manually set a faster shutter speed to freeze action. If your subjects have slight movement, setting it to around 1/125th of a second is ideal, but for more stability, go higher.

This feature is useful, especially for photographing kids or similar scenarios, and it's recommended to explore and customize based on your needs.

If your camera isn't stabilized, set the shutter speed to around 1/60th of a second. Adjust it faster or slower based on your needs. When using a tripod in aperture priority mode, you can control motion blur by changing the shutter speed. In video mode, aperture priority is like Program Auto, but switch to manual mode for creative control.

Manual mode

Now, let's try using manual mode on the camera. In manual mode, three boxes are at the bottom of the screen. You can tap them with your finger to make changes or use the dials.

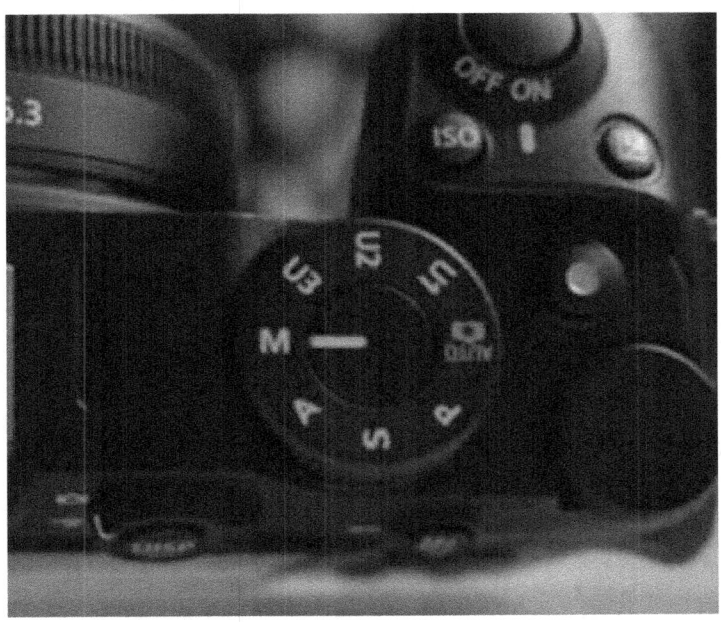

The front dial adjusts how much light comes in, the back one controls how fast the picture is taken, and the ISO can change automatically or be set by you. In manual mode, you'll see a live preview of your photo. If it looks too dark, increase the ISO or slow down the shutter speed to let in more light. You can check the histogram to ensure the exposure is balanced for a good photo.

Switch to manual mode if your camera's shutter speed is too slow at 1/10th of a second, especially for capturing fast movement. Increase the shutter speed to around 1/400th of a second to freeze the action, making the photo darker. To compensate, raise the ISO, as you can't lower the F number further. With a shutter speed of 1/400th and ISO of 3200, you can now capture moving objects with better clarity. In manual mode, you have control over settings like Aperture to adjust the depth of field.

Manual mode in video

If you switch to video mode, you can enjoy full power. In this mode, you can turn off auto ISO while recording by adjusting the ISO settings to manual. For the best results, set the shutter speed to be twice the frame rate. For instance, if you're recording at 4K/24 fps, set the shutter speed to 1/50th of a second. If recording at 60fps, set it to 1/250th of a second.

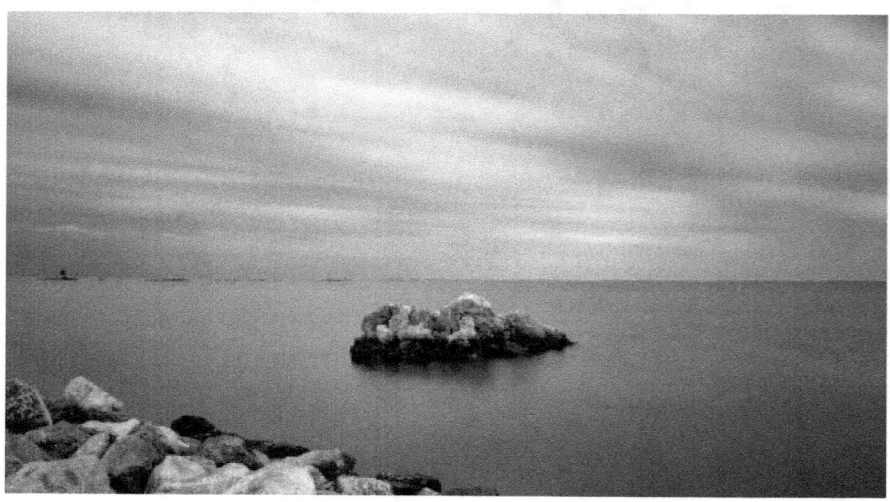

If your video looks too dark or bright despite having a good shutter speed, press the display button to see the histogram for a better view. Adjust the ISO to make the exposure right. For example, if you started with ISO 100 and it's too dark, switch to ISO 400. You can also control the depth of field by adjusting the Aperture, but be aware that it might make the scene darker. If you're recording video and don't want to change the shutter speed, consider raising the ISO to compensate for aperture changes.

CHAPTER 5: CAPTURING VIDEO

Recording Videos (auto)

To make a video easily, follow these steps:

1. Turn the selector to Movie shooting.
   - **Note:** You can't use Flash in video mode.
2. Switch to auto mode on the mode dial.
3. Press the video-record button to start recording.
   - The REC lamp will light up, showing that you're recording.
   - The monitor displays the time left for recording and tracks your subject's focus if you tap it.
   - Don't cover the microphone.
4. Press the video-record button again to stop recording.

Movie Shooting Menus

Reset the movie shooting menu

The "Reset movie shooting menu" option does exactly what it sounds like – it sets the Movie Shooting Menu back to how it was when you first got it. If you want to begin anew with all the Movie Shooting Menu settings, follow these steps:

1. Pick "Reset movie shooting menu."

2. Decide between Yes or No, then press OK.

File naming

You can change the first three letters (prefix) in a video's file name to something you like instead of the default "DSC." You can use your initials, a mix of letters and numbers, all letters, or all numbers. Open the file and choose the first three letters you want.

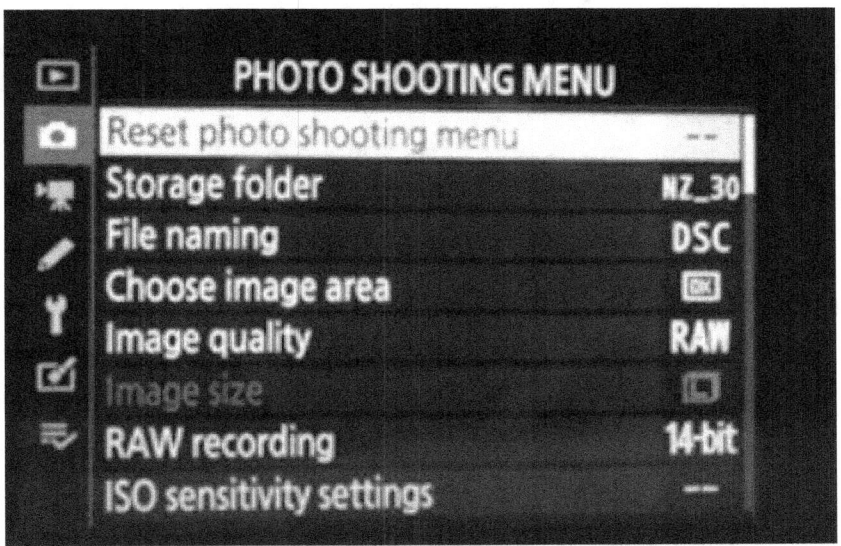

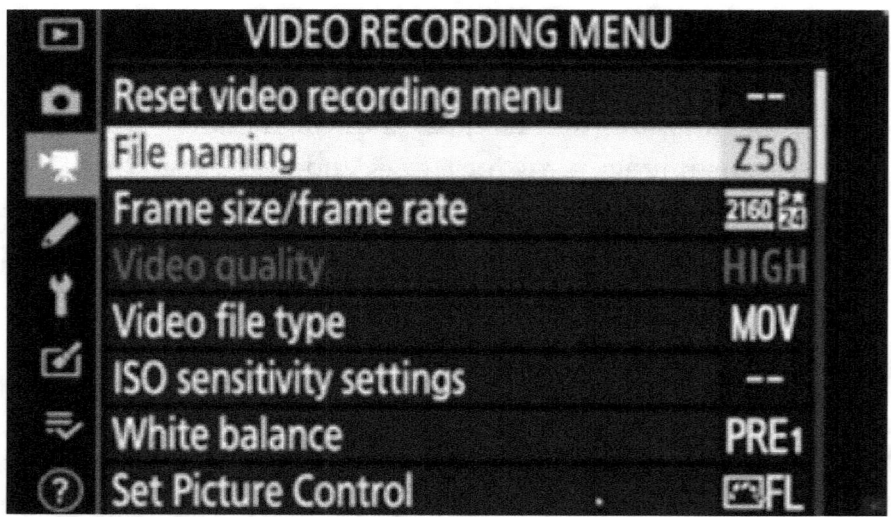

Follow these steps to set up your custom file naming characters.

1. Choose a name for your files.

2. Tap the screen to add a new starting part to your file names. Use the alphabet and numbers in the middle of the screen. Your chosen characters will show where the dark-gray cursor is in the name box (VID). Move left or right by tapping the arrows or selecting individual characters. When you're done, press OK or tap Zoom in to save.

86

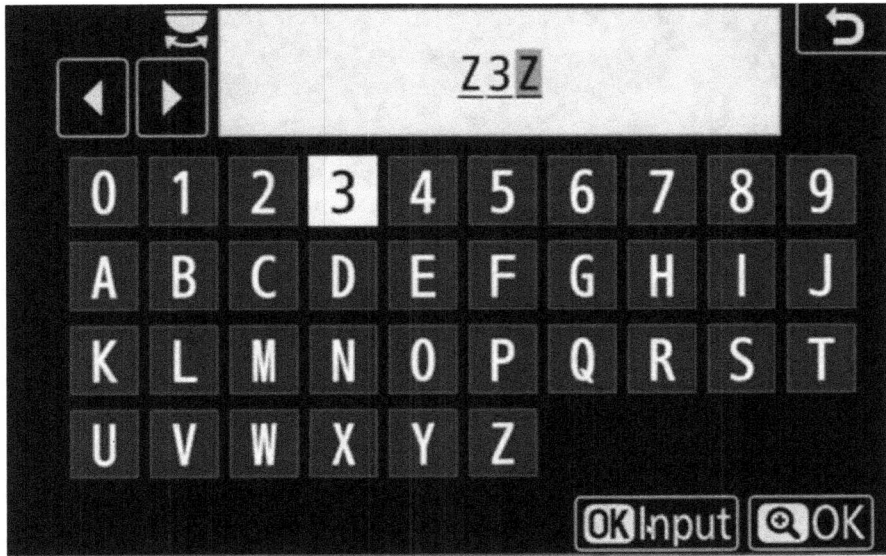

Your camera will now use "Z3Z" to start all video file names. The fresh start will be the first three characters in every image file name.

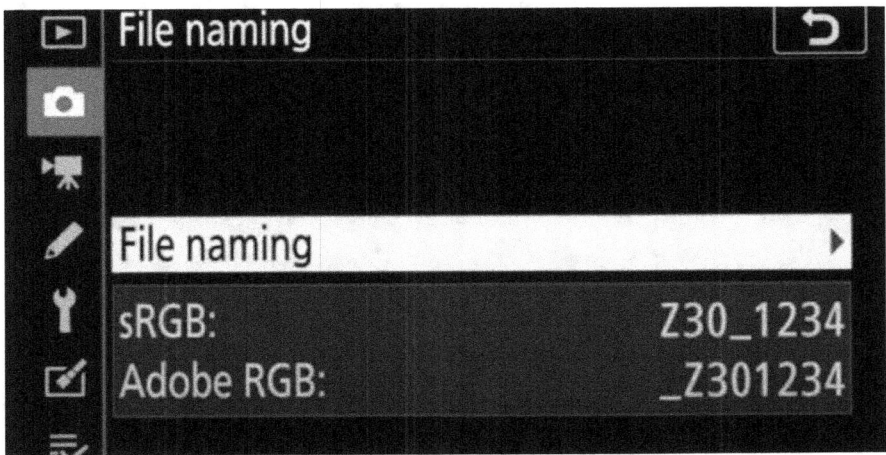

Frame size/frame rate

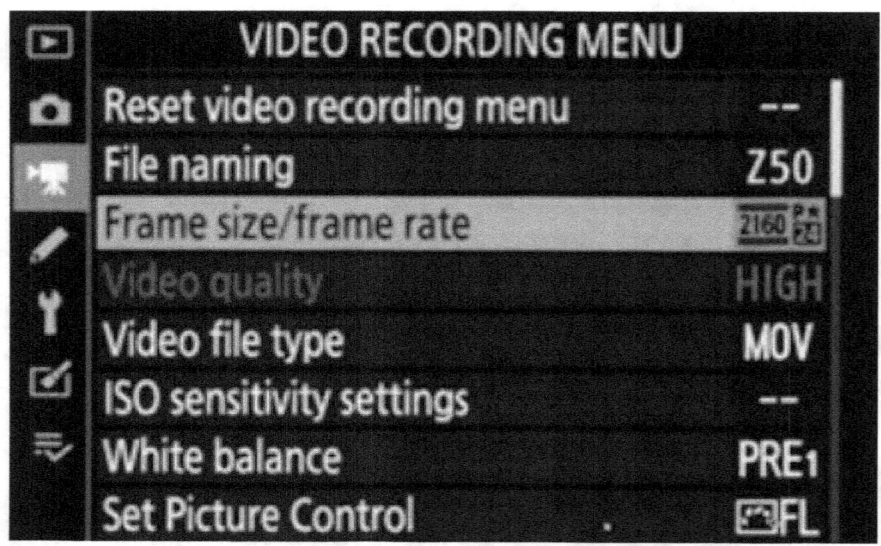

Pick the size (like 2160p or 1080p) and speed (120p, 100p, 60p, 50p, 30p, 25p, 24p, or slow-motion) using this function.

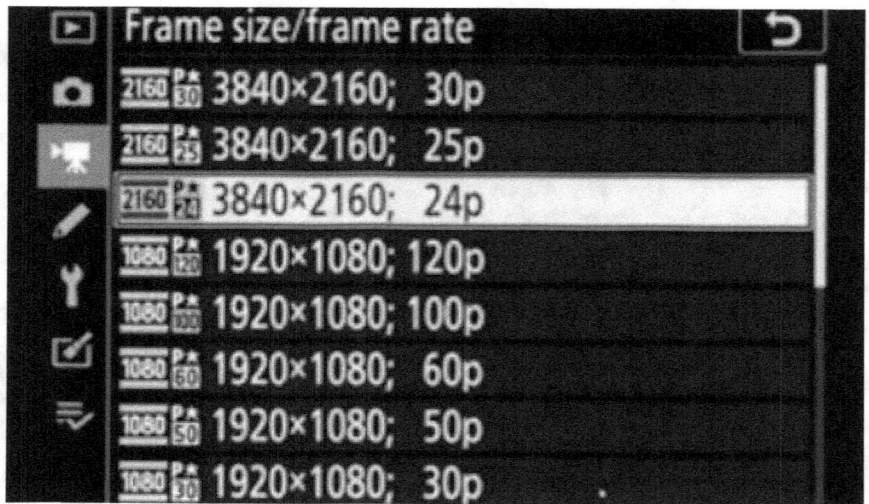

Video Quality

The movie's quality is determined by its "bit rate" or Mbps, similar to how the JPEG type (Fine, Normal, Basic) sets the quality of a still image. Higher bit rates mean better video quality. When saving video to the memory card, you can choose between High-quality and Normal bit rates, depending on the video's frame size and frame rate.

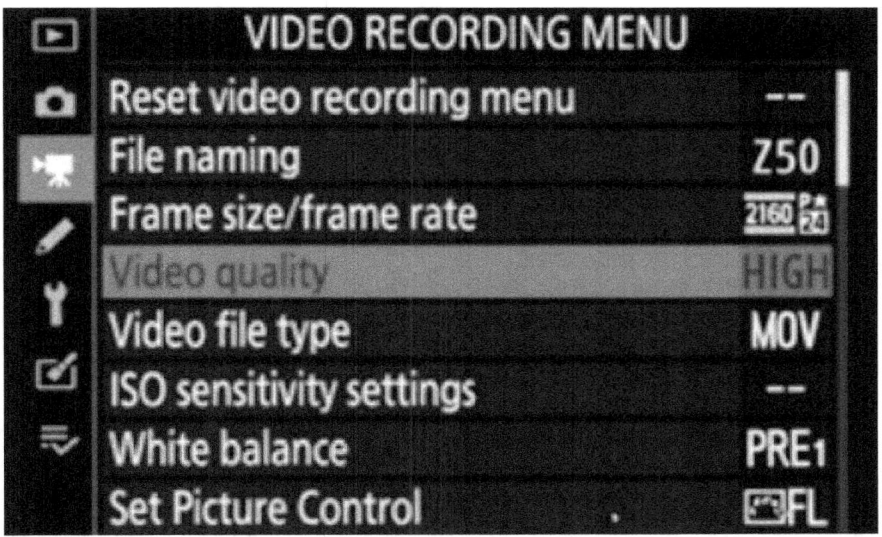

If the Movie quality option is grayed out, it's because you have one of the three 4K UHD (2160p) video modes selected, and in those modes, the camera always uses High quality.

To pick the quality of your movie, follow these steps:

1. Pick Video quality.
   Choose either High or Normal quality, then press OK.

2. Remember, this setting only affects videos saved on the camera's memory cards, not uncompressed video streamed through the HDMI port to an external recorder.

Note: You can also find this option in the I Menu. Just press the i button, and it's on the top row, second from the left, under Frame size and rate/Image quality.

Video file type

The Z30 usually uses MOV (Apple QuickTime) for videos, but you can also go with MP4, which is great for internet streaming and works well on most devices. MOV and MP4 work on almost all computer and smart device video players.

Pick your favorite movie file type by following these steps:

1. Select the movie file type.

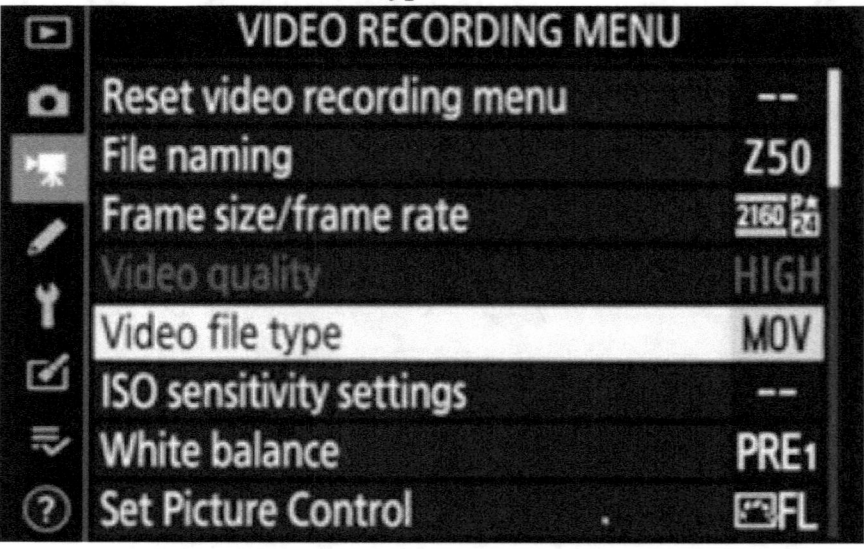

2. Decide between MOV or MP4 and click OK.

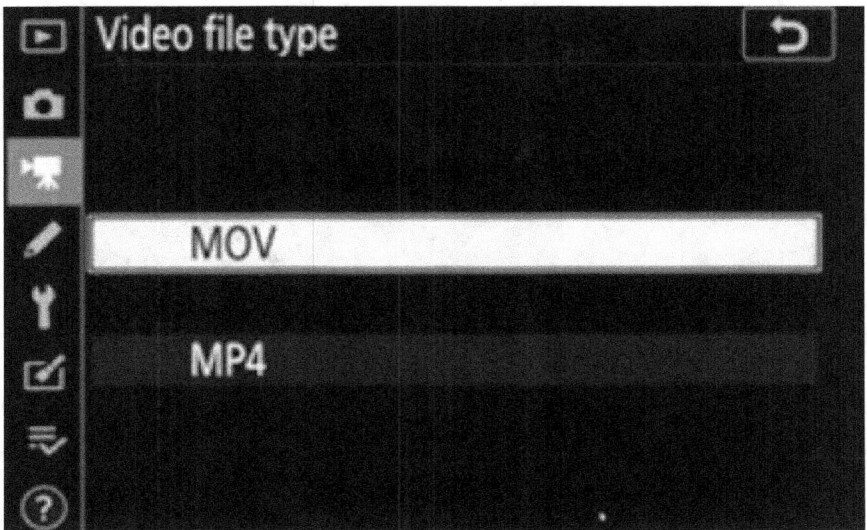

ISO sensitivity settings

Movie ISO sensitivity settings control how sensitive the camera is to light when recording a video. You can either set it yourself or let the camera do it automatically. It's important to let the camera adjust the sensitivity automatically, especially when the lighting changes, to avoid having too dark or bright videos. While you can keep the ISO setting constant in certain situations, it's generally better to let the camera adapt so you can focus on capturing the best videos.

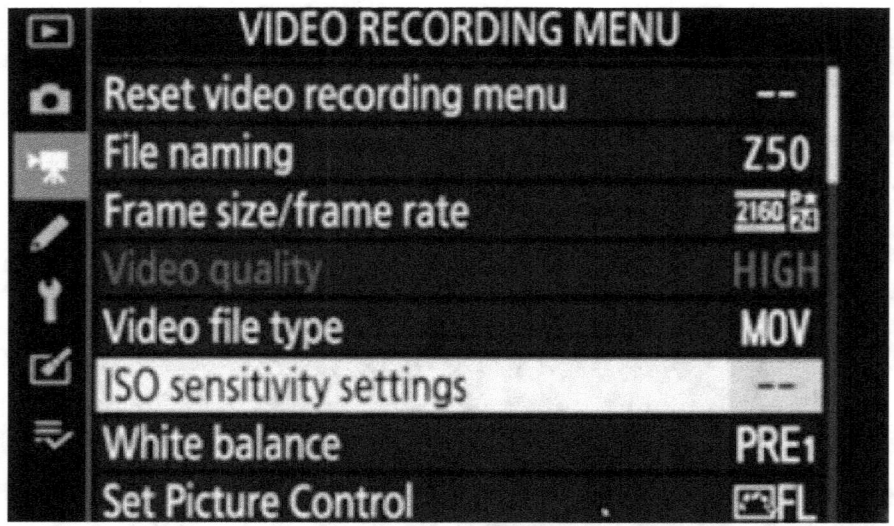

Maximum Sensitivity

The Maximum Sensitivity setting is like a safety feature for your camera. It lets the camera automatically adjust its sensitivity to light, ranging from a minimum of ISO 100 to whatever Maximum Sensitivity value you've chosen (up to ISO 25600). It means the camera can quickly adapt to different lighting conditions, ensuring your videos look good without worrying too much about adjusting settings. The camera aims to use the lowest ISO sensitivity possible for a good video, but it can quickly increase it to the Maximum Sensitivity level if necessary.

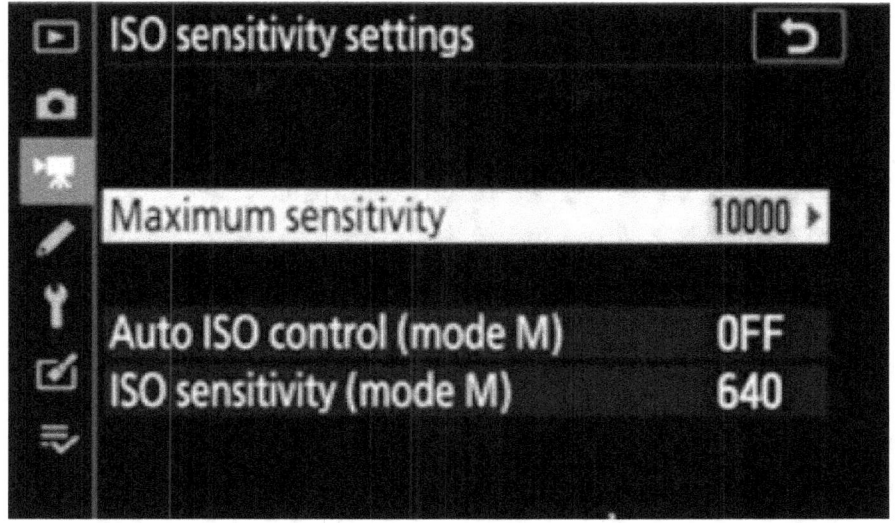

When your camera is set to P, S, or A modes for exposure, it automatically adjusts the ISO sensitivity for video. The highest ISO it can use is the one you set as the Maximum sensitivity, and the lowest is ISO 100. In manual mode (M), you can control ISO manually. To set the Maximum sensitivity for video:

1. Navigate to ISO settings > Maximum sensitivity on the screen.
2. Choose a maximum ISO value (e.g., 6400) for low light, then press OK.

Note: In P, S, or A modes, the camera doesn't consider Auto ISO or manual ISO settings from mode M.

Auto ISO Control (Mode M)

In manual mode (M), Auto ISO adjusts sensitivity automatically. If you're in auto modes (P, S, or A), it doesn't work. In manual mode, you can turn off Auto ISO and set your own ISO value in the settings.

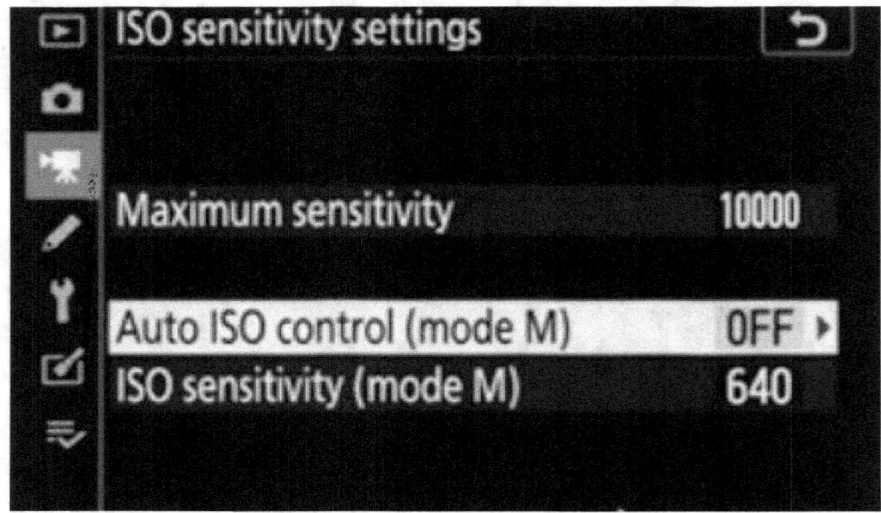

Auto ISO control in mode M lets you decide if you want the camera to automatically adjust ISO or if you prefer to do it manually. You might want manual aperture and shutter speed control while letting the camera handle ISO. Alternatively, you can manually turn off Auto ISO and control everything, including ISO sensitivity. Here's how to turn Auto ISO control (mode M) on or off:

1. Go through the screens by choosing ISO sensitivity settings, then Auto ISO control (mode M), until you reach the third screen.
   Decide if you want it On or Off, then press OK.

2. After turning on Auto ISO control (mode M), pick the highest ISO you want for shooting videos.

ISO Sensitivity (Mode M)

ISO sensitivity in Manual mode lets you pick a specific ISO value. But it doesn't do anything if you're in P, S, or A auto modes. The chosen ISO value affects your photo in one of two ways.

- **Auto ISO control (mode M) set to On:** The camera automatically picks the right ISO sensitivity for a good picture. If you set a specific value, like ISO 100, it won't pay attention to that.
- **Auto ISO control (mode M) set to Off:** When turned Off, the camera will stick to one ISO value. This ISO will only change during the entire video if you change it yourself.

To choose ISO sensitivity in Manual (M) mode, follow these steps:

1. Go through the screens by choosing ISO sensitivity settings, then ISO sensitivity in mode M, until you reach the third screen.
2. Check the list to see what changes when you switch Auto ISO control in mode M On or Off. If you pick Off, scroll in the ISO sensitivity menu until you find the ISO value for your video, then press OK. You can pick any value from ISO 100 to 25600.

White balance

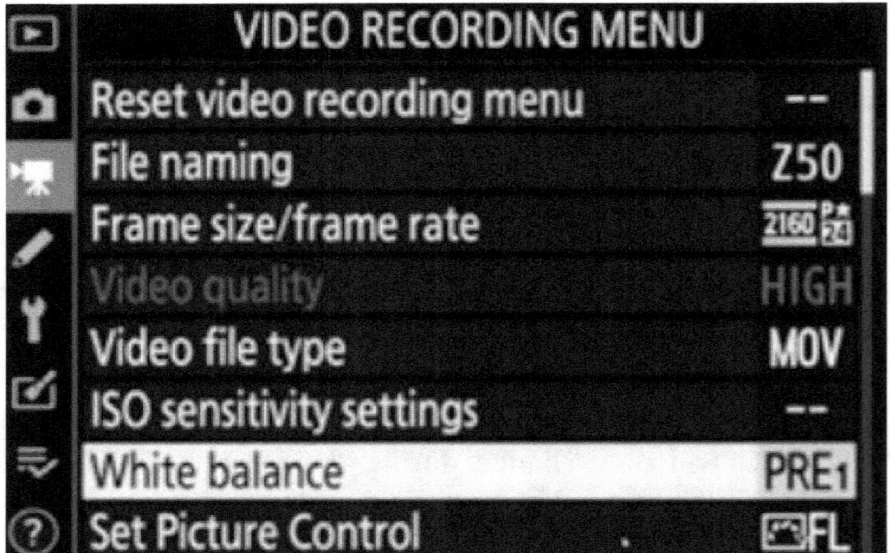

The White Balance settings in video recording are similar to those for photos. You can choose a location like Direct sunlight or Auto or a specific color temperature. You can use a white or gray card to set the best color temperature if you want precise colors..

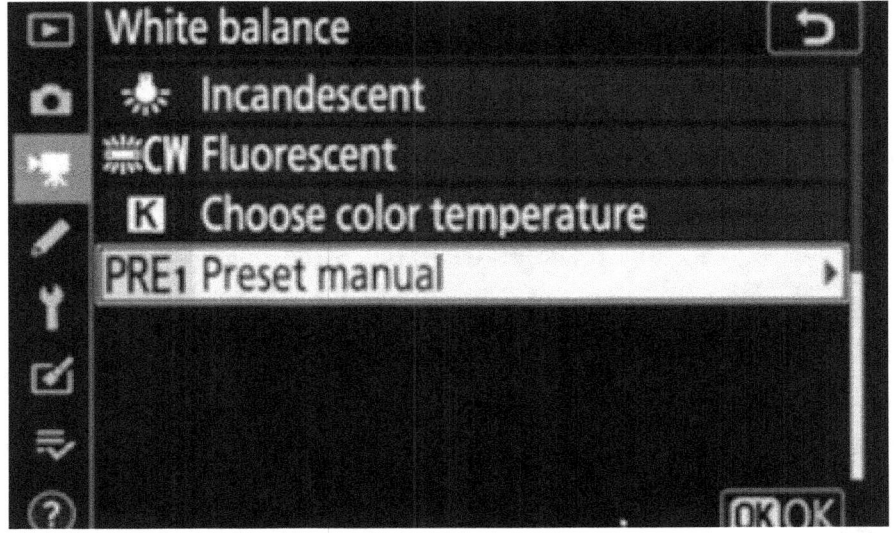

Set Picture Control

Set Picture Control will ensure you successfully pick a style for your videos. You can use the same style you chose for photos or select from the preset styles Nikon provided. Each style has settings like Sharpness, contrast, brightness, saturation, and hue that you can adjust.

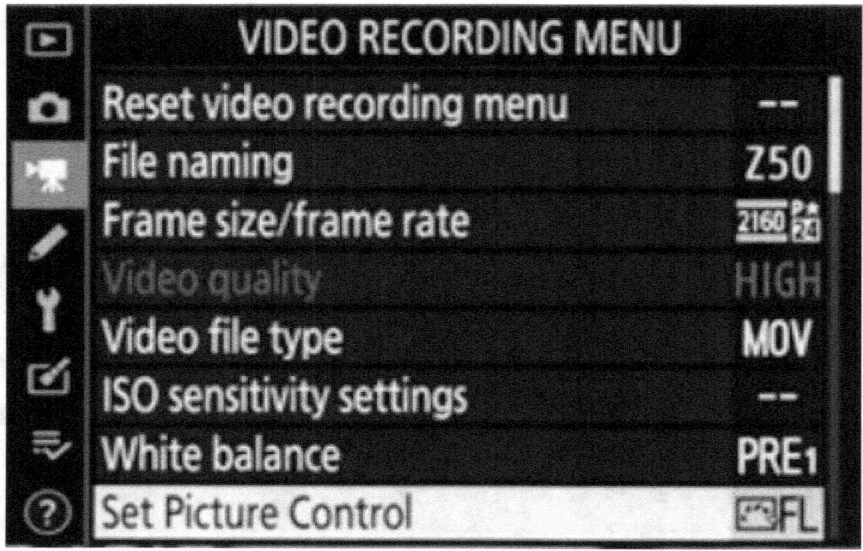

A quick sharp setting also combines Sharpness, mid-range sharpening, and clarity. The default setting is the same as the last one you used for photos.

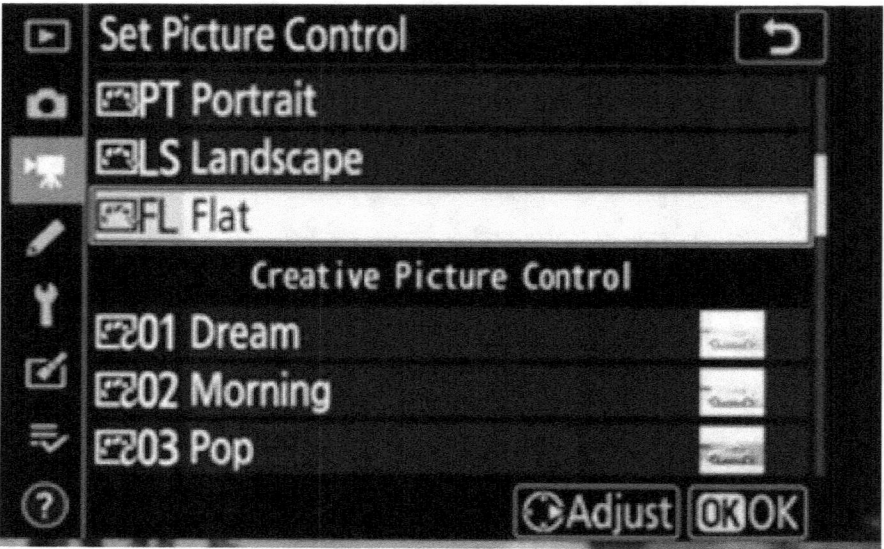

- **Same as photo settings:** It uses the same picture settings as the last time you took photos, like when you first got the camera.
- **A Auto:** Uses a basic picture setting but tweaks it for better portraits and landscapes. It makes skin tones softer for faces and enhances colors for plants and the sky in landscapes, similar to a vivid setting but not as intense. Other things look like the standard setting.

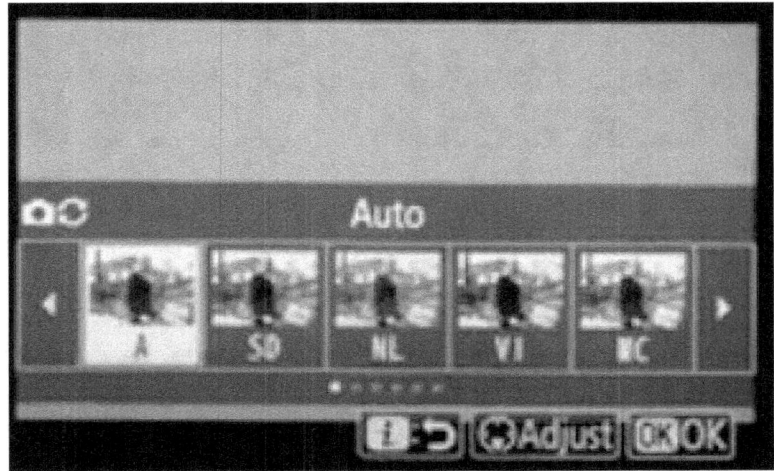

- **SD Standard:** Choose a Picture Control with moderate Sharpness, balanced Clarity, Contrast, Brightness, Saturation, and Hue. It's a versatile setting for videos, not too vibrant and not too muted in color.

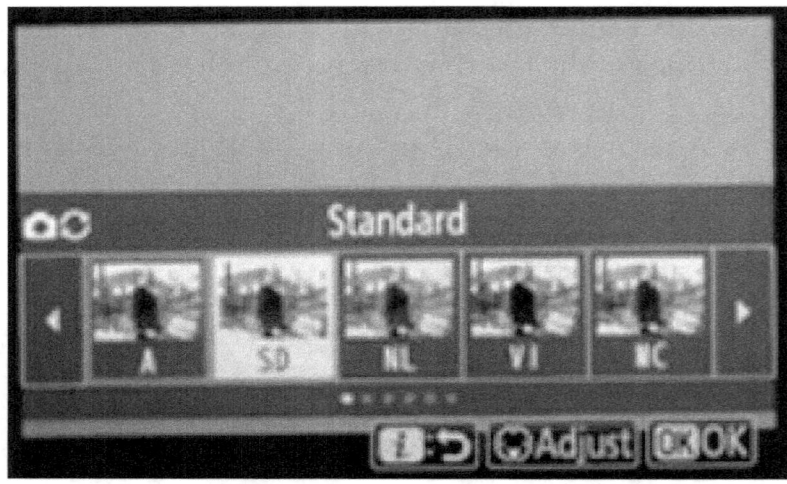

- **NL Neutral:** Choose a Picture Control with a little sharpening, medium clarity, contrast, brightness, saturation, and hue. It works well for videos with subjects that need less color and contrast.

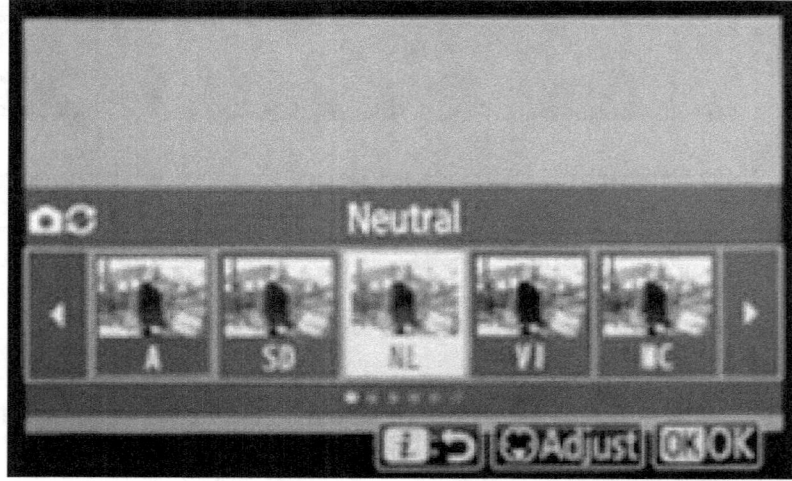

- **VI Vivid:** Choose the "Vivid" Picture Control setting for nature videos if you want vibrant reds, blues, and greens with high Sharpness and contrast. However, avoid using it for videos with essential skin tones as it enhances colors and contrasts strongly.

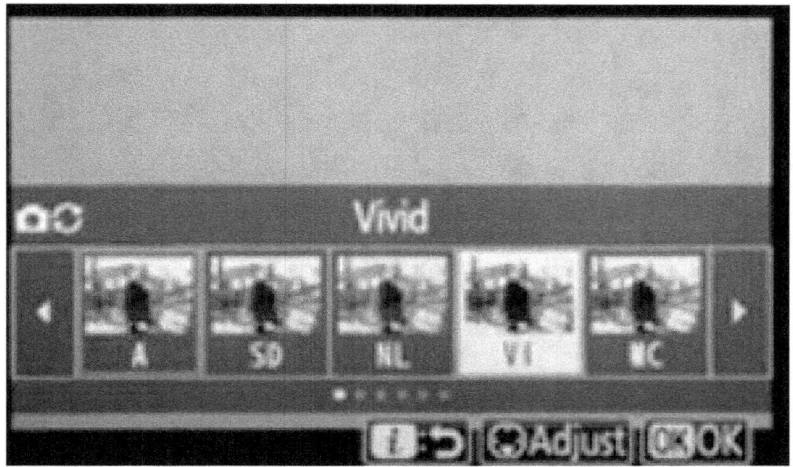

- **MC Monochrome:** A Picture Control for fans of classic black-and-white videos. It has standard medium settings, but you can play around with the contrast. For cool effects, you can also add filter effects like yellow, orange, red, or green. Plus, there are toning options like B&W, sepia, cyanotype, and more to give your video attractive tints.

101

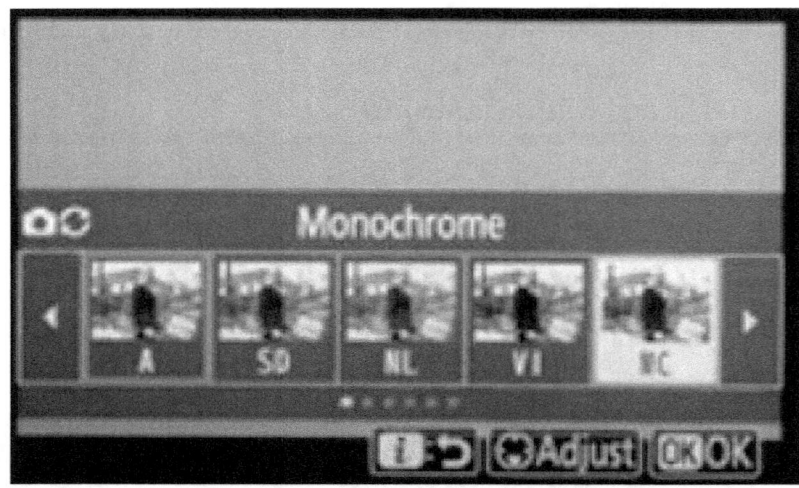

- **PT Portrait:** This Picture Control is great for videos with people, focusing on skin tones. It's more colorful and has higher contrast than NL Neutral, but less intense than SD Standard and less vibrant than VI Vivid.

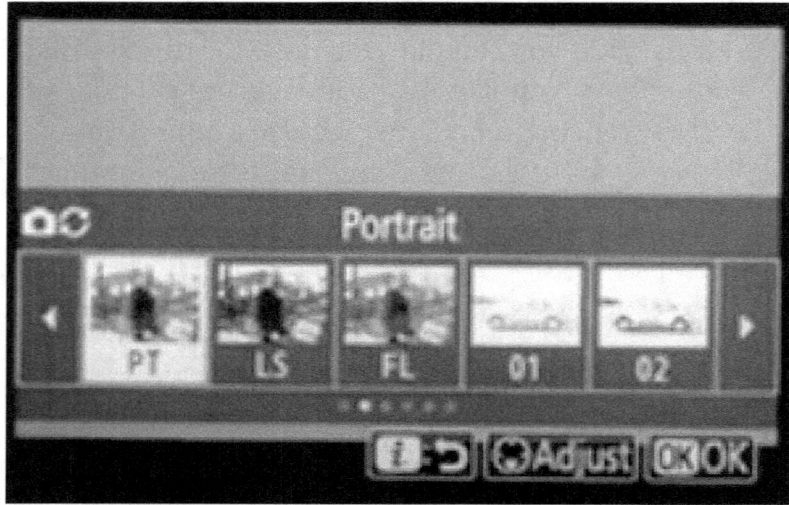

- **LS Landscape:** This Picture Control is for people who like natural-looking landscape videos without the extra vividness of the VI Vivid control. It adds more color to natural hues but could be more brightly and colorful.

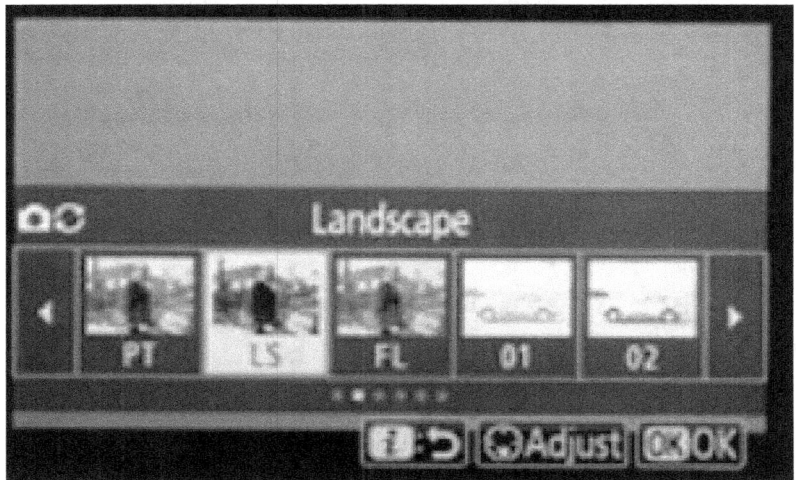

- **FL Flat:** This setting is made for severe video makers. It keeps the video natural with less Sharpness, contrast, and color intensity. This way, when you edit the video using professional software like Final Cut Pro X or Adobe Premiere Pro CC, you can choose how much Sharpness, contrast, and color you want to add.

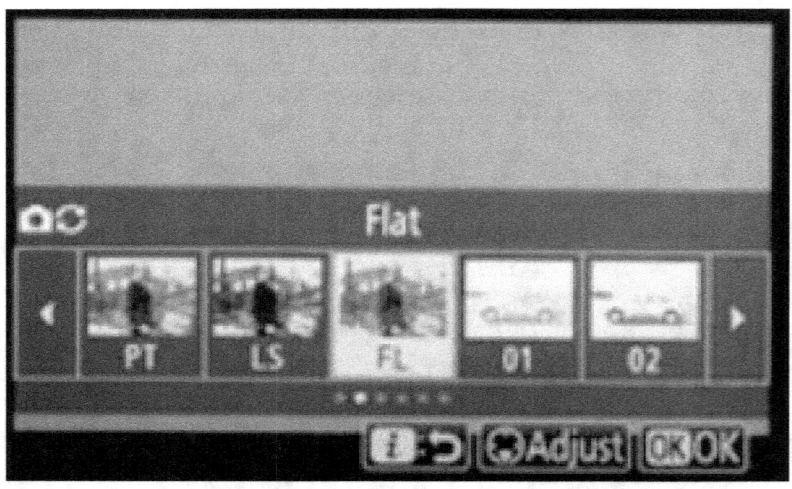

Manage Picture Control

Manage Picture Control lets you make and save your custom settings for future videos. You can tweak existing Nikon or Creative Picture Controls and give them a new name. If you make changes using the Set Picture Control function, it's a one-time thing. But if you want to create custom controls, the Z30 can do that for you.

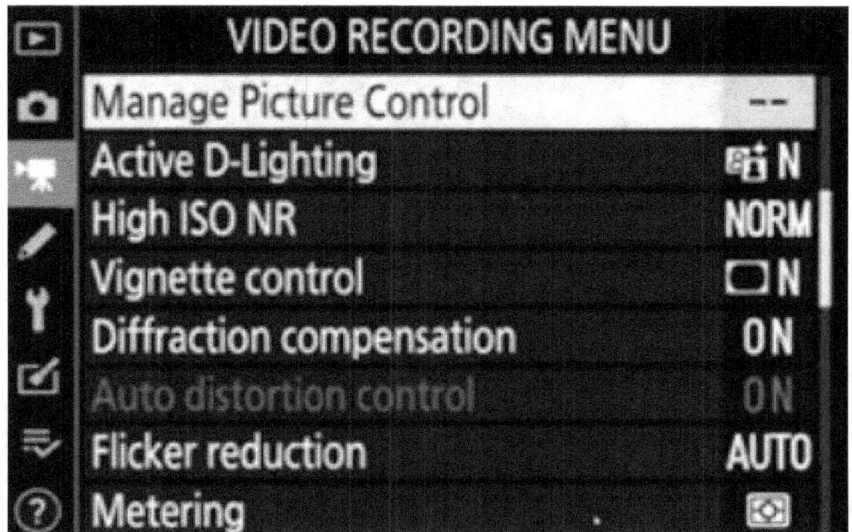

If you adjust a Nikon Picture Control in this setting, it only changes how your videos look. The camera keeps different Picture Controls for photos and videos. So, changes you make for photos won't appear in the video settings, and vice versa.

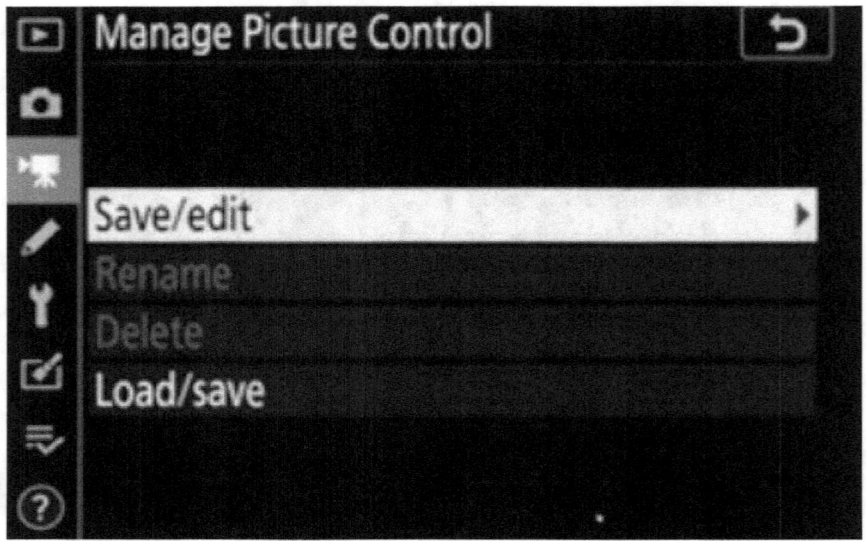

Save/Edit a Custom Picture Control

To change and save Picture Control settings for your videos, follow these steps:

1. Go to Manage Picture Control.
2. Choose Save/edit, then scroll right.

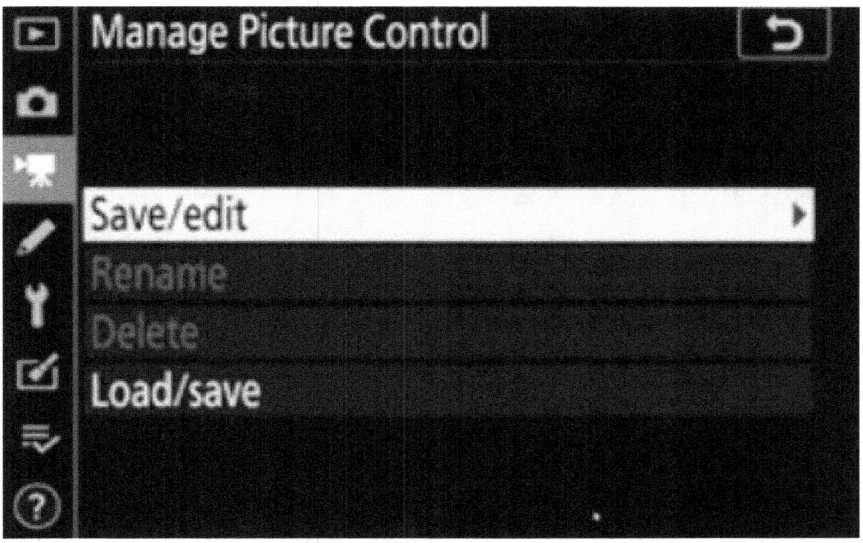

3. Pick a Picture Control as a starting point, like SD Standard. Modify and save it with a new name.

4. Adjust Sharpening, Contrast, etc. I used Quick Sharp and added +1 for more Sharpness (out of 2). Press OK when done. To cancel changes, press Delete or tap Reset for factory settings.

5. Pick one of the nine storage areas called C-1 to C-9 and swipe right. You can only see seven of them without scrolling down. Save up to nine different Custom Picture Controls here for later use with Set Picture Control.

6. Now, you'll see the Rename screen. It works like screens you've used to rename things before. Type a new name by tapping characters in the center, and they'll show up where the dark-gray cursor is (like Standard-02). Use left/right arrows in the top-left to move across the name. Tap the Aa& button in the lower-right corner to switch from uppercase to lowercase. If you mess up, place the dark gray cursor over the mistake and choose Delete.

When the name is ready, press OK to save it. "Saved" will briefly show on the Monitor. The camera might create a default name by adding a dash and two numbers to your current control name. I kept it as STANDARD-02.

7. Tap OK to finish.

Rename a Custom Picture Contro

Here's how to rename a Custom Picture Control for video:

1. Go to Manage Picture Control.
2. Select Rename.
3. Choose the Custom Picture Control you want to rename (C−1 to C−9). Let's say we're renaming STANDARD-02.
4. On the Rename screen, type the new name by tapping on the characters in the center. Use the left/right arrows to move within the name and Aa& button to change the case. If you make a mistake, use Delete. Once done, press OK to save (max 19 characters). I renamed STANDARD-02 to STANDARD-EX2.
5. Press OK to finish.

Delete a Custom Picture Control

To remove a video Custom Picture Control, do these steps:

1. Go through the screens by selecting Manage Picture Control, then Delete until you reach the third screen.
2. Pick one of your nine Custom Picture Controls and choose the one you want to delete (like VIVID-02).
3. Confirm the deletion by selecting Yes at the prompt that asks if you want to delete the Picture Control, then press or touch OK.

Load/Save a Custom Picture Control

Here are three options in the Load/Save menu:

1. Brings Custom Picture Controls from the memory card into your camera. You can save up to nine controls in your camera's memory (C1–C9).
2. Shows a list of Custom Picture Controls on the memory card. You can choose and delete them individually.
3. This lets you copy your Custom Picture Controls (C1–C9) from your camera to a memory card. This way, you can share them with others. The camera can display up to 99 control locations (01–99) on one memory card.

Active D-Lighting

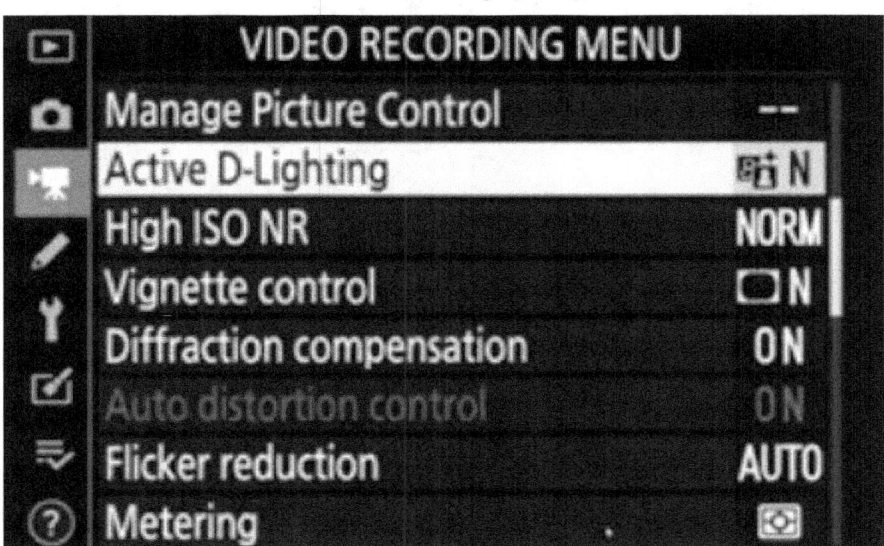

Active D-Lighting helps you adjust the contrast in your videos. If shadows are too dark, you can make them brighter to see more detail. If the highlights are too bright, you can make them slightly dimmer to keep more facts in those bright areas.

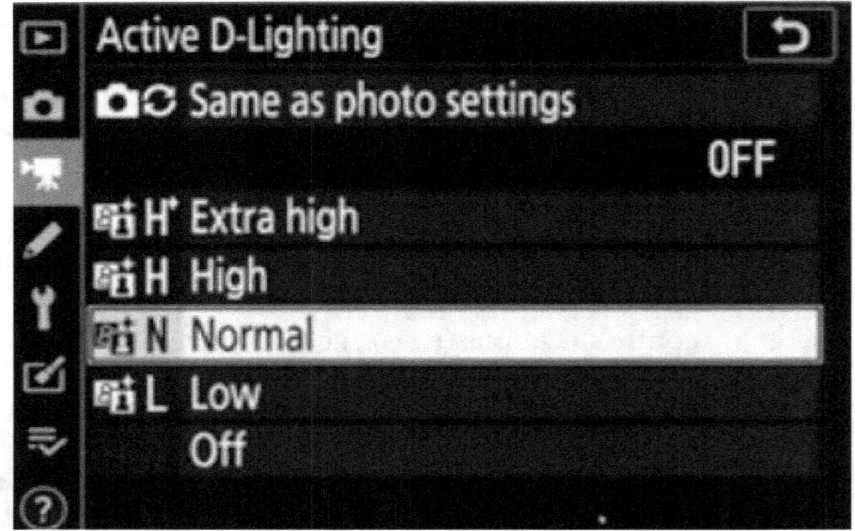

High ISO NR

High ISO NR helps reduce graininess in your videos when you use high ISO settings. The Z30 camera handles noise well, providing clean videos at ISO 3200. Even with High ISO NR off, some noise reduction still occurs, and you can adjust the level using settings like High, Normal, Low, or Off.

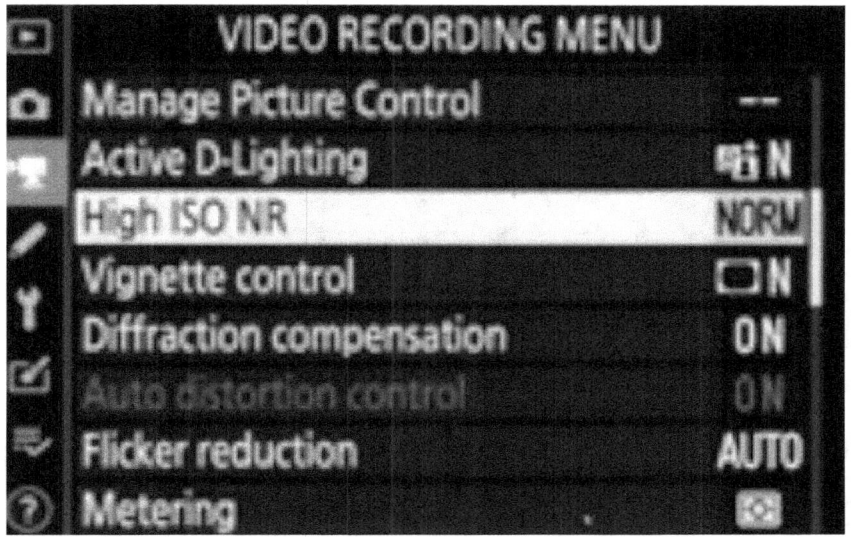

Vignette control

Vignette control helps lessen the dark corners in photos caused by some lenses. When light hits the edges of the camera sensor, it's at a steeper angle than in the center. It can darken at the extreme edges, especially with wide apertures. Nikon's Vignette control setting reduces this effect for specific Nikkor lenses, making your photos look more even.

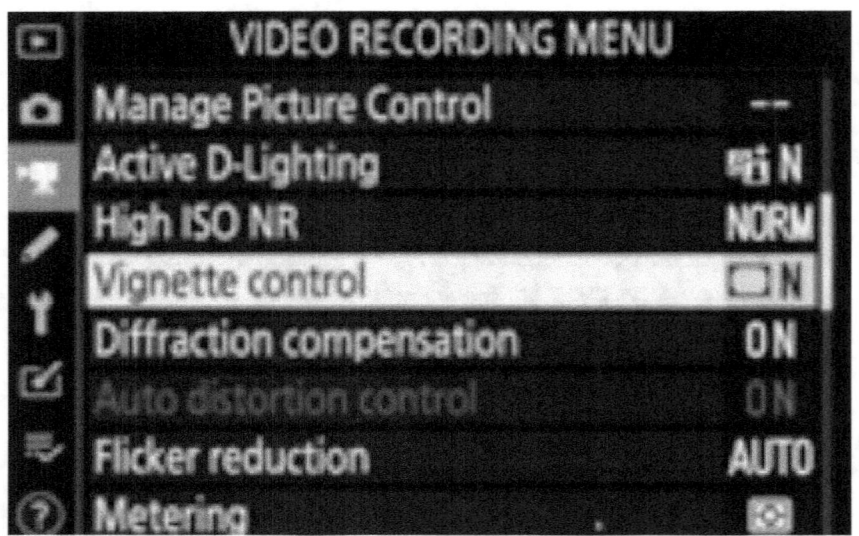

Auto distortion control

Auto distortion control automatically fixes bending and squeezing distortions in your videos. It works well for architectural photographers who want straight lines. Use it with specific lenses but not with others like fisheye lenses. If the option is grayed out, your camera likely corrects distortion without this feature so you can ignore it.

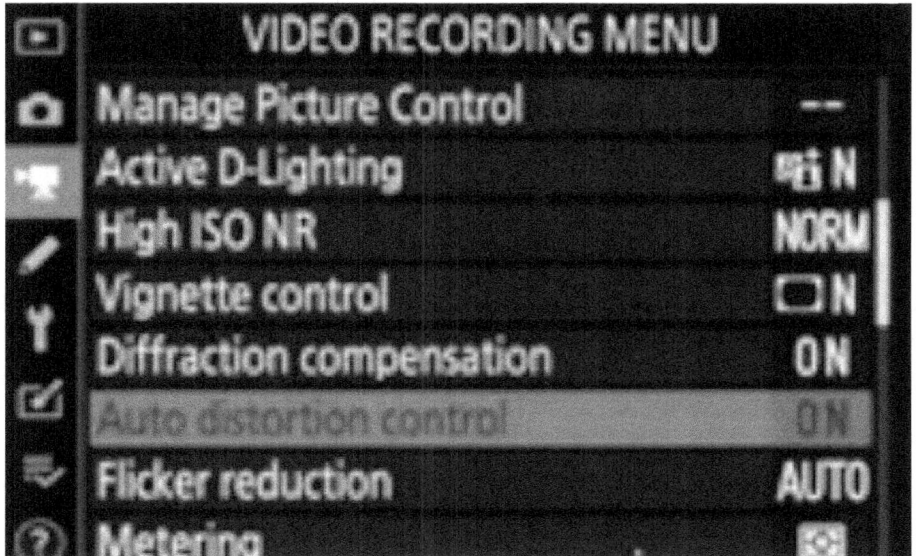

Flicker reduction

Flicker reduction helps prevent those dark bands we sometimes see in videos. When you record video in specific lightings, like fluorescent or mercury-vapor lights, your video might show these bands (flicker). To use this:

1. Click on Flicker reduction.

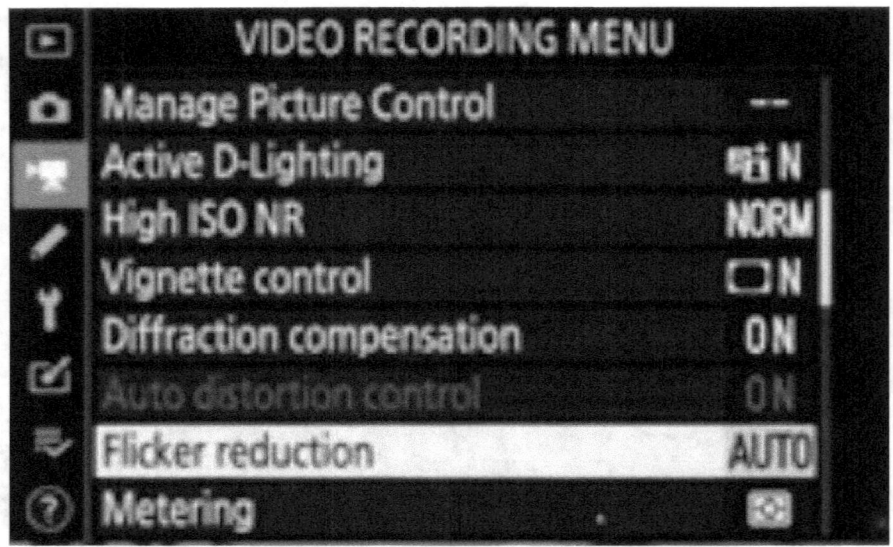

2. Start with Auto mode, and if it doesn't work well, try 50Hz or 60Hz settings for better results.

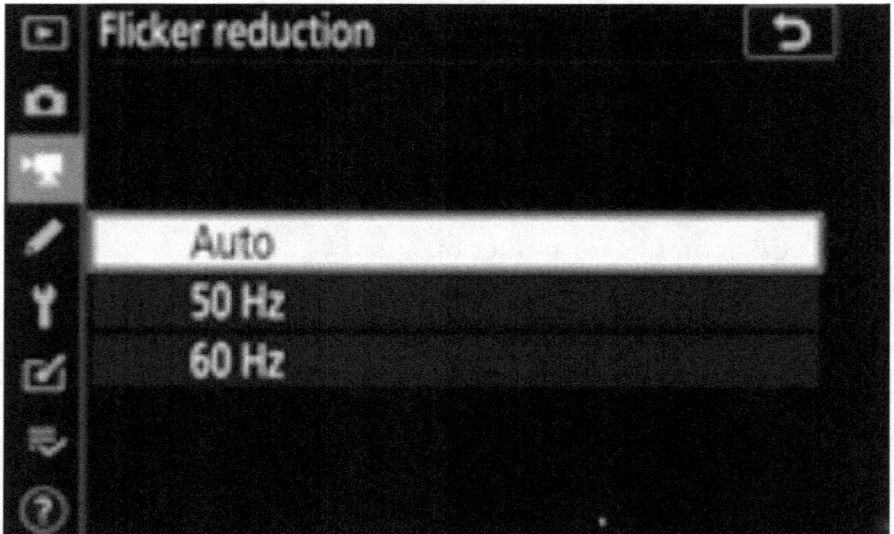

3. If the video is too bright, use a smaller aperture like f/8.

Optical VR

Optical VR, or in-lens vibration reduction, helps prevent blurriness caused by shaky hands while holding the camera. When using a Nikkor lens with Optical VR, the camera and lens cooperate to minimize vibrations, allowing you to shoot stable videos without additional stabilizing equipment. There are two VR modes and an Off option, each serving different purposes.

On Normal: Use this mode when taking pictures of things that aren't moving much. It works well if you're holding the camera, walking, or recording something that could be moving faster.

SPT Sport: This setting is great for capturing fast-moving sports or subjects. When you're following the action (panning), the Z30 turns off horizontal movement stabilization but still helps with vertical movement. When the issue stops, stabilization works again for both horizontal and vertical motion.

Off: The camera turns off the image stabilization for Z-mount lenses.

Electronic VR

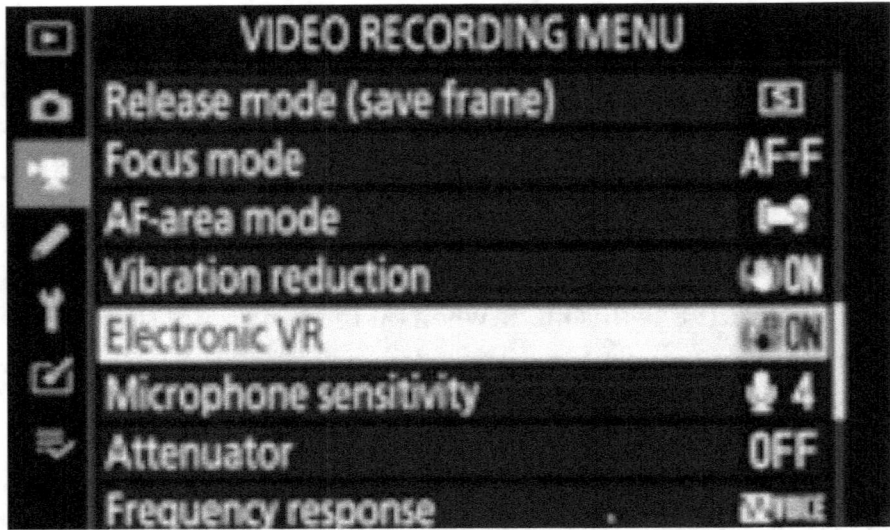

Electronic VR helps steady your videos when you're shooting without a tripod. It's different from the physical sensor-shifting technology in some cameras. Instead, Electronic VR adjusts the video frame by shifting pixels to reduce the impact of minor camera movements, working together with in-lens Optical VR for added stability.

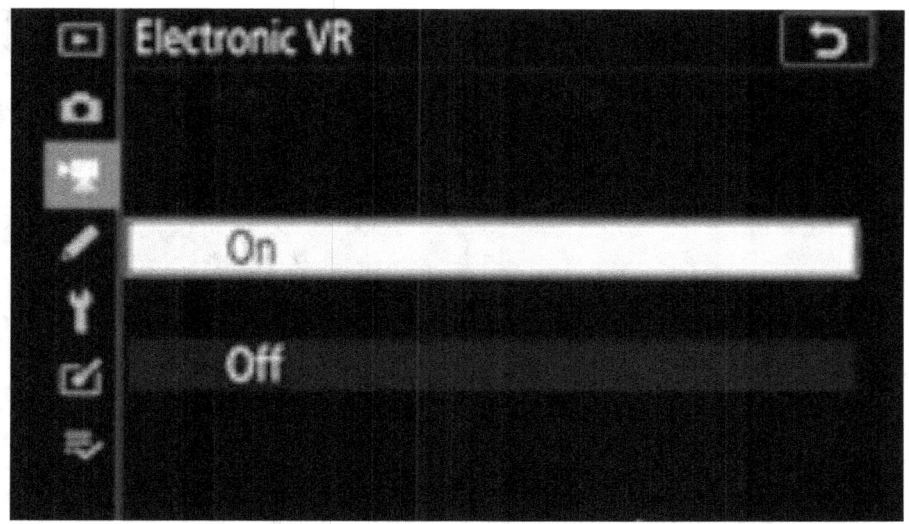

Attenuator

The microphone Attenuator is like a helper that changes how sensitive the microphone is based on how loud things get. Imagine recording a sports game, and when there's a loud cheer after a score, the Attenuator makes the microphone less sensitive so it doesn't get too noisy. To turn it on or off, follow these steps:

1. Pick Attenuator.

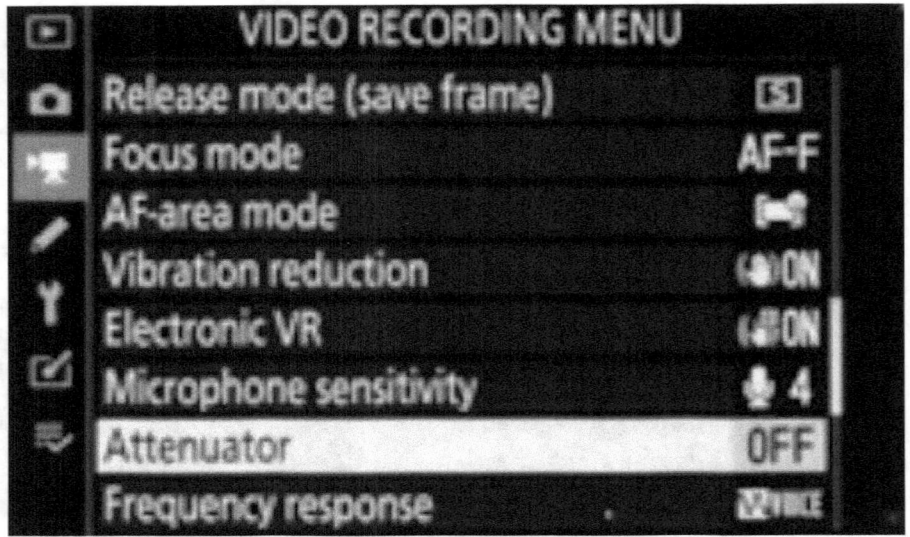

2. Decide if you want it on or off, then press OK.

Frequency response

The Frequency Response Function helps you pick the right audio settings for recording video. You can choose specific ranges to capture the sounds you want, like birdsong in the jungle or a lecturer's voice while avoiding unwanted noises like footsteps or road traffic. Good sound is crucial for high-quality video recording!

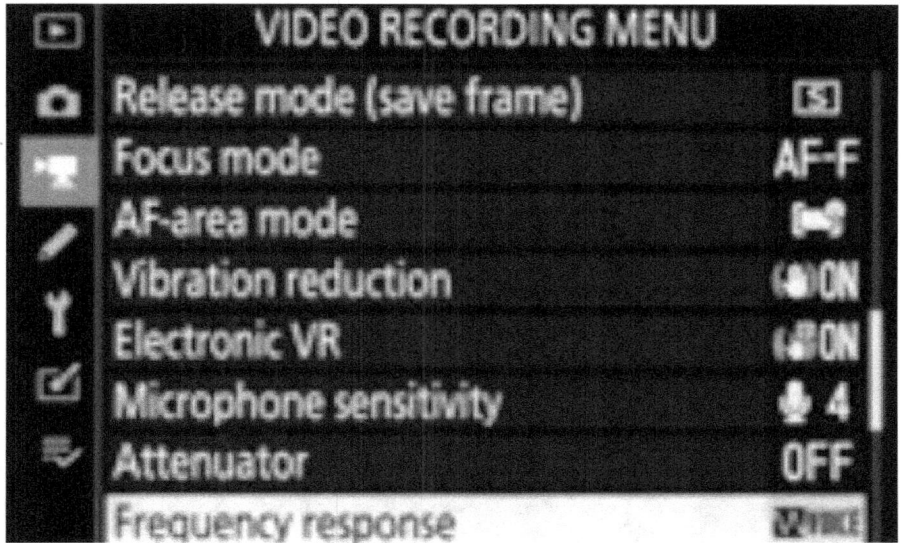

Wind noise reduction

The Wind noise reduction feature helps eliminate annoying wind sounds when it hits the camera's built-in microphones. Remember, it won't work if you use an external microphone – only with the mic built into the camera.

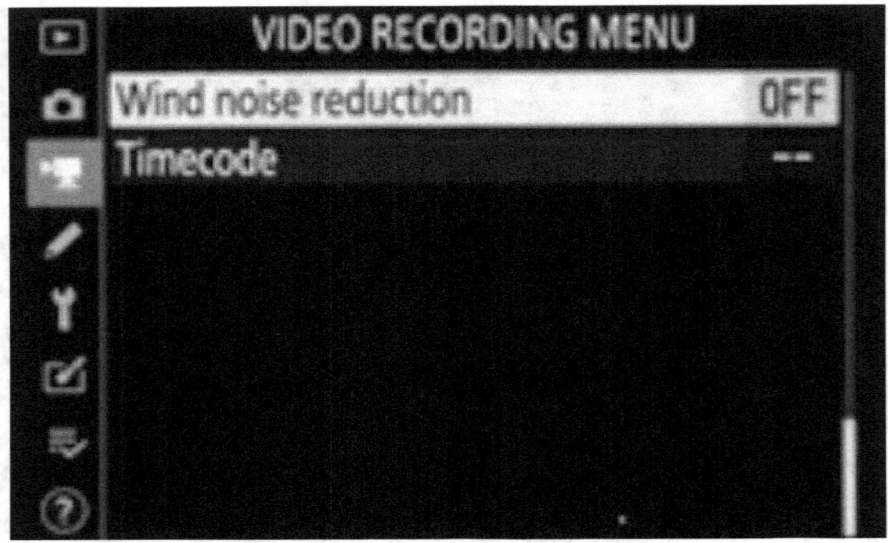

Have you ever filmed a video on a nice, windy day and then realized later that instead of the clear sound you wanted, there's this rumbling wind noise on your recording?

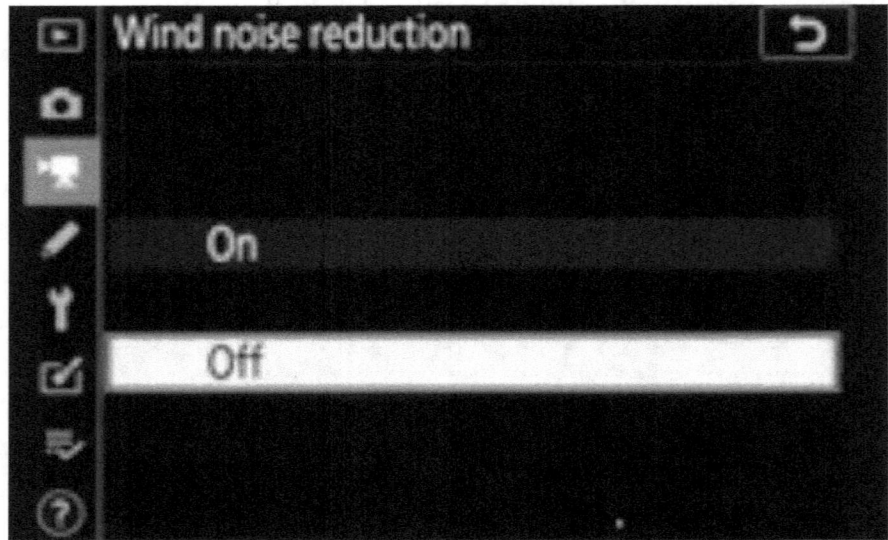

Even though you might still hear some of it without special external microphones, this feature can make a big difference by reducing those low-frequency wind noises.

CONCLUSION

W e've come to the end of the Nikon Z30 User Guide. We hope that you have enjoyed this guide and that you have learned a lot about your new camera.

Now that you have learned how to use your camera like a pro, you can go out and take stunning photos and videos. We encourage you to experiment with different settings and modes to find what works best for you. We also encourage you to join online communities and forums where you can connect with other Nikon users and share your photos and experiences.

We hope that you are happy with your Nikon Z30. It's a great camera that can take amazing photos and videos.

www.ingramcontent.com/pod-product-compliance
Lightning Source LLC
Chambersburg PA
CBHW062327290526
45794CB00005B/1925